Weapons of the War

CONTENTS

Page	Topic
4	Introduction
6	The Ukraine War
12	Ukrainian military organisation and Order of Battle
16	Russian military organisation and Order of Battle
20	AK-74 Rifle
22	Machine Guns
24	Heavy Machine Guns
26	Other Small Arms
28	Anti-Tank Weapons / Stugna-P
29	Anti-Tank Weapons / Javelin
30	Anti-Tank Weapons / NLAW
31	Anti-Tank Weapons / 9M133 Kornet
32	Anti-Tank Weapons / MT-12 Rapira
33	Anti-Tank Weapons / Panzerfaust 3
34	Anti-Tank Weapons / RPG
36	Armour / T-64
38	Armour / T-72
40	Armour / T-80
41	Armour / T-90
42	Western Tanks
44	M-55S
45	Older Soviet Tanks
46	BMPs
48	BTRs
50	Western Armoured Fighting Vehicles
52	MRAPs
53	Technicals
54	MTLB
55	Soviet-era AFVs
56	Tigr
57	Engineer Vehicles
58	Artillery – HIMARS/MLRS
60	Artillery – BM-27-30
61	Artillery – RM70
62	Artillery – BM-21 Grad
64	Artillery – 2S19
65	Artillery – 2S1 Gvozdika
66	Artillery – 2S7 Pion
67	Artillery – 2A36 Giantsint-B
70	Artillery – Krab
71	Artillery – Caesar
72	Artillery – M109
73	Artillery – FH-70
74	Artillery – DANA
75	Artillery – M777
76	Aircraft – MiG-29
78	Aircraft – MiG-31
79	Aircraft – Su-27
80	Aircraft – Su-34
81	Aircraft – Su-25
82	Aircraft – Mi-8
83	Aircraft – Ka-52
84	Aircraft – Mi-24
85	Aircraft – Mi-28
86	Anti-Aircraft Systems – ZU-23-2
87	Anti-Aircraft Systems – 2K22 Tunguska
88	Anti-Aircraft Systems – Pantsir
89	Anti-Aircraft Systems – Tor
90	Anti-Aircraft Systems – S-300
91	Anti-Aircraft Systems – Patriot
92	Anti-Aircraft Systems – NASAMs
93	Anti-Aircraft Systems – MANPADS
94	Unmanned Systems – Bayraktar
95	Unmanned Systems – Shahed
96	Unmanned Systems – Eleron
97	Unmanned Systems – Orlan-10
98	Unmanned Systems – Small Drones
100	Unmanned Systems – Tupolev 141/143
101	Unmanned Systems – Ukrainian Drone Boats
102	Loitering Munitions – Switchblade
103	Loitering Munitions – Lancet
104	Missiles – Iskander
105	Missiles – Kinzhal
106	Missiles – Kh-101
107	Missiles – Kalibr
108	Missiles – Neptune
109	Missiles – Storm Shadow
110	Electronic Warfare
111	Mines
112	Mine Clearing
113	Naval Power – Russian Black Sea Fleet
114	Glossary

TOP: A Ukrainian T-64BM fires it main gun. Note the reactive armour blocks on the side and the recoil has rocked the tank back on its suspension. (US ARMY)

ABOVE: Smoke and dust fly as Ukrainian troops fire a US-supplied M777 155mm howitzer in May 2022. (UKRAINIAN MOD)

LEFT: This Russian T-80BVM was captured and placed into service by the Ukrainian 93rd Mechanised Brigade. This sub-model is among the more capable tanks on Ukraine's battlefields. (UKRAINIAN MOD)

ISBN: 978 1 80282 976 1
Editor: Chris Miskimon
Senior editor, specials: Roger Mortimer
Email: roger.mortimer@keypublishing.com
Cover Design: Steve Donovan
Design: SJmagic DESIGN SERVICES, India
Advertising Sales Manager: Brodie Baxter
Email: brodie.baxter@keypublishing.com
Tel: 01780 755131
Advertising Production: Becky Antoniades
Email: Rebecca.antoniades@keypublishing.com

SUBSCRIPTION/MAIL ORDER
Key Publishing Ltd, PO Box 300, Stamford, Lincs, PE9 1NA
Tel: 01780 480404
Subscriptions email: subs@keypublishing.com
Mail Order email: orders@keypublishing.com
Website: www.keypublishing.com/shop

PUBLISHING
Group CEO and Publisher: Adrian Cox

Published by
Key Publishing Ltd, PO Box 100, Stamford, Lincs, PE9 1XQ

Tel: 01780 755131
Website: www.keypublishing.com

PRINTING
Precision Colour Printing Ltd, Haldane, Halesfield 1, Telford, Shropshire. TF7 4QQ

DISTRIBUTION
Seymour Distribution Ltd, 2 Poultry Avenue, London, EC1A 9PU
Enquiries Line: 02074 294000.

We are unable to guarantee the bona fides of any of our advertisers. Readers are strongly recommended to take their own precautions before parting with any information or item of value, including, but not limited to money, manuscripts, photographs, or personal information in response to any advertisements within this publication.

© Key Publishing Ltd 2024
All rights reserved. No part of this magazine may be reproduced or transmitted in any form by any means, electronic or mechanical, including photocopying, recording or by any information storage and retrieval system, without prior permission in writing from the copyright owner. Multiple copying of the contents of the magazine without prior written approval is not permitted.

www.keymilitary.com

Weapons of the Ukraine War

Welcome

ABOVE: Tracer rounds ricochet into the night sky as Ukrainian BMP-2s fire their 30mm 2A42 autocannon. (US ARMY)

The Ukraine War is the largest conflict in Europe since World War II. The effects of this war are global, as both Ukraine and Russia are supported by allies and carry out campaigns which affect the global economy. This special edition looks at the weapons in use during this conflict. Media coverage often focuses on advanced systems such as the US HIMARS rocket launcher, the UK's Storm Shadow missiles, or the Russian Kinzhal missile. This war, like all others, is a combination of the old and the new.

Weapons by necessity tend to be durable; with proper storage and a modicum of maintenance they will last decades. The weapons of the Ukraine War exemplify this; we see the latest missiles in use alongside small arms from World War II. There are reports of conscripts from the breakaway Luhansk and Donets Republics, allied with Russia, being given hundred-year-old Mosin-Nagant bolt action rifles. Simultaneously, photographs show Ukrainian Territorial Defence Force troops carrying the same weapon in its sniper configuration.

This mix of old and new is evident in the Ukraine War. Most weapons in use are either Soviet-era holdovers or updated versions of systems originally designed in the Soviet era. The Soviets habitually placed old weapons into long term storage and both combatants possess many of these old stockpiles in their territory. Soviet weapons of all types serve in both armies, partly because many are still effective or upgraded, but mainly because neither nation ever had the financial means to replace them all.

Both nations also benefit from foreign assistance. Ukraine receives a vast array of weapons and equipment from abroad, mostly from NATO members. There is practically no major weapon type, from small arms to combat aircraft and missiles, Ukraine has not received, along with the requisite spare parts, ammunitions and training. This provides firepower, versatility and increased capability while simultaneously complicating logistics, maintenance and ammunition resupply.

Russia has also gotten assistance from friendly states, though fewer in number than those assisting Ukraine. Iran has provided Unmanned Aerial Systems (UAS), such as the Shahed 136 drone. South Korean authorities state

WEAPONS OF THE UKRAINE WAR

LEFT: A USAF airman loads pallets of Javelin missiles in their shipping containers at Dover Air Force Base in February 2022. Both sides use extensive foreign aid. (USAF)

The vast variety of weapons in use in the Ukraine War precludes our being able detail all of them. Within these pages are a mix of the major systems, those in widespread use, and a few which are simply interesting. We hope the reader will be informed by this showcase of the weapons in use and the information gathered on their employment in this dreadful conflict. As far as possible we have used imagery of the weapons in the hands of the combatants. This occasionally includes still shots taken from video and drone footage. While that sometimes means a reduction in image quality, we feel it gives the reader a better sense of the weapons in actual field use.

Both combatants and their supporters produce extensive amounts of reports, social media stories and propaganda. This must be expected during wartime. We have done our best to present the most accurate information possible. Readers are encouraged to look at the vast amount of information available elsewhere but remember much of it is coloured by the loyalties of the creator.

While the focus here is on weapons systems, there are no wonder weapons that will win this war for either side. HIMARS, Storm Shadows and Kinzhals have been proven potent in combat, but none have proven or will prove decisive. The weapons in these pages are only effective due to the determination, skill and ingenuity of their users.

Christopher Miskimon
Major, Field Artillery, USA (Ret)
Editor

LEFT: A common image from the Ukraine War: a rusted, destroyed tank, covered in graffiti. (US DOD)

BELOW: Neither side has been able to attain air superiority in this war, due to effective integrated air defence systems. Here, a Russian surface-to-air missile flies from its launcher. (RUSSIAN MOD)

North Korea is suspected of providing small arms, artillery, ammunition and missiles, though the North Korean government denies providing any aid to Russia. China has not provided weaponry, but Russia has purchased body armour, non-military drones and thermal imaging devices. The Japanese news organisation Nikkei published a report in June 2023 stating their study of customs clearance information indicates Russia is re-purchasing military equipment it previously sold to several nations.

Both nations have shown great ingenuity in modernising and employing old weapons. This conflict has shown how quickly weapons and munitions of all kinds are used up in the maelstrom of modern combat.

Thousands of tanks, armoured vehicles, artillery pieces and other equipment have been destroyed during the war. Attempts to count them, such as on the Dutch open-source website Oryx, are valuable for general measurement but can only provide a rough estimate of losses. Not every destroyed or damaged weapon is photographed or recorded for social media posting.

Further, even weapons which appear badly damaged may be recovered and repaired. Loss numbers mentioned in these pages are at best estimates based on available information.

www.keymilitary.com 5

THE WAR

The Ukraine War

Europe's largest conflict since World War II

RIGHT: Soldiers of the Ukrainian 72nd Mechanised Brigade fire an Iranian-made mortar. This weapon was one of thousands captured by the US Navy from a shipment of weapons being smuggled to the Houthis in the Middle East. (UKRAINIAN MOD)

BELOW: Soldiers of the Ukrainian 79th Airmobile Brigade breach a wire obstacle. Penetrating an enemy defensive position is one of the most dangerous tasks for infantry. (US ARMY)

The War in Ukraine is the most significant conflict of the 21st Century thus far. The Russian invasion, which began 24th February, 2022, took the world largely by surprise despite the massing of Russian troops along the Ukrainian border and warnings from intelligence agencies. The world was equally surprised by how effectively Ukraine's forces resisted the much larger and better equipped Russian military.

The war began in 2014, when Russia invaded and occupied the Crimean Peninsula in a swift and relatively bloodless operation after supporting a campaign of pro-Russian demonstrations. A month later a Russian-instigated uprising in the Donbas led Ukraine into essentially a civil war against the self-named Donetsk and Luhansk People's Republics (DPR and LPR). Their forces were armed partly from Ukrainian depots and partly by Russia.

Ukraine's military, starved of funding and hampered by Russian sympathisers, struggled to effectively respond. However, thousands of citizens formed volunteer units and joined the war; by late August 2014 they were pushing close to the Russian border, only to be pushed back by direct Russian intervention.

A ceasefire agreement followed, but the conflict continued to simmer at a reduced level.

Ukraine began a wide-ranging effort to reorganize, improve and train its military for the next round in this war. It received extensive aid from NATO, concerned over the threat of a resurgent Russia on its eastern flank. NATO tactics, organisation and training helped the Ukrainians in their effort to create a military which could fight effectively. Likewise, Russia continued its own series of reforms, which were hampered by corruption but did make strides. The DPR and LPR were rearmed with second-rate weapons and kit.

In hindsight the Russian invasion in 2022 seems a disastrous mistake, but from Russian President Vladimir Putin's view it was a valid if risky option. Russian operations in and attempts to control nations on the Russian periphery were tolerated by the West. Further, prior military operations in Chechnya, Georgia and Syria provided successes that highlighted some of the Russian military's improvements while masking persistent shortcomings. Before the 2022 War, Russian information operations focused on purported cries for help from Donetsk and Luhansk, as well as the supposed control of Ukraine by fascists and neo-Nazis.

WEAPONS OF THE UKRAINE WAR

ABOVE: Ukrainian soldiers pick through the wreckage of a Russian armoured column in Bucha in the early months of the war. Stalled columns proved vulnerable to artillery and tank hunting teams.
(UKRAINIAN GOVERNMENT)

Russian forces massed on the border under the pretence of 'exercises,' and while many thought the crisis would be resolved, others, including many intelligence agencies, warned the threat was real after studying Russian troop movements and military financial activities, which indicated the Russians intended action.

The war began in the predawn hours of 24th February, 2022, with a prerecorded declaration by President Putin, who called the invasion a 'special military operation.' Jamming, cyberattacks and missile bombardments started within 45 minutes. Air strikes were limited and met some Ukrainian resistance. Nine Russian field armies and two corps from the LPR and DPR advanced into Ukraine.

A major part of the Russian plan involved a quick strike on the Ukrainian capital of Kyiv to topple the government and kill or capture its President, Volodymyr Zelenskyy. The Spetsnaz special forces units previously infiltrated into Kyiv for this purpose failed, while a heliborne assault to

LEFT: Russian armour advances toward Kyiv in the war's early days. The crews are watching for ambushes by enemy anti-tank teams.
(RUSSIAN MOD)

THE WAR

ABOVE: One of the most common images in this war is a view of an artillery strike from a scouting UAS. Drones enable artillery to fire quick, accurate fire missions. (UKRAINIAN SECURITY SERVICE)

RIGHT: A Russian tank crosses the Seversky Donets River in April 2022. Ukraine has many sizable rivers, making bridging equipment a vital necessity. (RUSSIAN MOD)

seize the Antonov Airport in Hostomel, northwest of Kyiv, ran into fierce resistance but reached its objective. Once there the debarking Russian paratroopers received help from the son of an airport employee to solidify their position. Meanwhile several battalions of ground troops advanced from Belarus to surround the city.

Ukrainian artillery and air strikes cratered the runway, making it useless for follow-on airlifts of reinforcements. Hard fighting followed over the next few days while approaching Russian columns became stuck in long traffic jams and were subjected to damaging attacks by Ukrainian soldiers and volunteers. The Russians soon withdrew from Kyiv, unable to take the city.

Around Kharkiv in northeastern Ukraine, the advancing Russian columns ran into one problem after another. Poor vehicle maintenance, communication failures, logistics difficulties and roving bands of Ukrainian troops all contributed to defeat. At Sumy, the Russians failed to secure an abandoned Ukrainian base, so 400 local civilians armed themselves from its stocks and drove the Russians back.

Another firefight broke out when a Ukrainian unit was spotted trying to pass through Russian lines. The Ukrainian unit managed to destroy 25 armoured vehicles of a Russian Battalion Tactical Group (BTG), while losing seven of their own. When elements of a Russian brigade, reinforced by Spetsnaz troops, entered Kharkiv the outnumbered Ukrainian defenders let the Russians get deep into the city before launching a counterattack which wiped out the Spetsnaz and a BTG; only a few dozen survivors escaped.

In the east and southeast the Russians and their DPR/LPR Allies made better gains, aided by the open terrain. Despite heavy casualties, the Russians managed to take Mariupol and Kherson though they fell short of reaching Odessa. In Mariupol, Ukrainian troops made a long stand around the Azovstal steel mill, lasting until mid-May.

With these opening blows and the effective Ukrainian defence, the war was now a general conflict instead of the quick operation the Russians wanted. Nevertheless, Putin refused to call off the operation and the war continued; his forces around Kyiv and Kharkiv withdrew for employment in the south and east. Ukraine received thousands of foreign citizens as volunteers, many of them with prior military experience. Contrastingly, Russia brought in Chechen troops. The Russians also became the subject of intense investigations into war crimes and human rights abuses.

The war became marked by successes and setbacks for both sides. Russian missile strikes on

WEAPONS OF THE UKRAINE WAR

LEFT: LeftInformation operations are a major part of the war as both sides try to control the outgoing narrative. This Ukrainian camera team is escorted by a group of soldiers. (UKRAINIAN MOD)

Ukrainian cities caused widespread civilian casualties and damage to infrastructure but were increasingly blunted by an improving Ukrainian air defence network. It also prevented the Russian Air Force from achieving air superiority, though Russian air defences achieved the same effort on the smaller Ukrainian air force. On 13th April, the Russian cruiser *Moskva*, flagship of the Black Sea Fleet, sank after reportedly being struck by two Ukrainian antiship missiles.

Russia began a second offensive on April 18, which caused extensive damage but made little headway. In September, a Ukrainian counteroffensive freed significant territory in the northeast around Kharkiv and cut off Russian supply lines at Lyman. In the south, Ukrainian forces liberated Kherson and all territory west of the Dnipro River, while the Russians fell back to the east bank. By the end of 2022, Ukraine had retaken half the land previously occupied by the Russians, leaving about 14% of the country in Russian control.

In response, Russia declared a partial mobilisation and moved to annex the occupied territories. Many Russians fled the country rather

BELOW: Russian airpower has been a major advantage despite the effectiveness of Ukrainian air defences. Planes such as these Su-34s are effective for ground attacks. (RUSSIAN MOD)

www.keymilitary.com

THE WAR

ABOVE: The Russian Cruiser *Moskva* was lost early in the war, but Russia's Black Sea Fleet has remained a major threat to Ukraine's coastline. (RUSSIAN MOD)

BELOW: Russia's airborne forces are among their most effective troops. These troops are taking part in the seizure of Antonov Airport outside Kyiv in February 2022. (RUSSIAN MOD)

than face conscription. The Wagner mercenary group was also committed to battle.

A few months of winter stalemate ended with a Russian winter offensive in February-March 2023. This attack also did not achieve a breakthrough and the fighting soon revolved around a siege of Bakhmut, which caused an estimated 100,000 Russian casualties, including 20,000 killed. The Russian government denied the numbers while Wagner leader Yevgeny Prigozhin called the figures accurate. He further noted many of those killed were drafted Russian convicts and complained of a lack of support from the Russian military. By late May the Russians captured Bakhmut after a bloody campaign.

On 6th June, 2023, a breach in the Nova Kakhovka dam caused extensive flooding in southwest Ukraine. Both sides blamed the other for the event. On 23rd June, Yevgeny Prigozhin claimed Russian regular forces shelled his troops and announced a march on Moscow against, notably, the Russian military leadership. Wagner forces captured Russia's southern headquarters in the city of Rostov-on-Don and were declared traitors. A convoy of Wagner troops, including armoured vehicles, drove halfway to Moscow. The next day a negotiation resulted in Prigozhin accepting effective exile to Belarus while his troops stood down. Prigozhin died in a plane crash on 23rd August.

Later in June, a long-awaited Ukrainian counteroffensive began, pushing east around Bakhmut toward Donetsk and south through Zaporizhzhia, which leads toward Crimea. This offensive gained little, as it struggled against Russian defensive positions situated behind thick minefields. The Russians also made use of their greater airpower and increasing numbers of UAS and loitering munitions.

In return, Ukraine made small gains on the ground but succeeded in attacks on ships of the Black Sea Fleet, long range UAS attacks on targets inside Russian territory, and successful missile attacks on the bridges to Crimea. On 22nd September 2023 Ukraine struck the Black Sea Fleet Headquarters in Sevastopol. By November, the Ukrainian offensive was over and the battlefield situation reached stalemate.

Russian offensives began in late 2023 and continued into 2024. In general, the Russian attacks achieved little, but by mid-February 2024 intense fighting around Adiivka resulted in the first Russian victory since Bakhmut the previous year. This success came at a high cost in troops and equipment for both sides, though as the attacking force, Russian losses are estimated to be significantly higher.

The Ukraine War is notable for several reasons. It has seen the

10 WEAPONS OF THE UKRAINE WAR

proliferation of UAS across the battlefield, including loitering munitions, drone boats and long-range systems. Tens of thousands of UAS are used by each side, with many of those lost or spent each month. The war points towards the need for modern militaries to develop inexpensive, mass-produced UAS for strikes, reconnaissance and electronic warfare.

Neither side has been able to achieve air supremacy, though the Russians have a larger air force more able to act over the battlefield, but it has taken losses. This points to effectiveness of each nation's Integrated Air Defence Networks (IADS), which have kept enemy planes mostly at a distance and shown reasonable effectiveness against massed missile and UAS attacks. Both sides have been able to use aircraft for strike missions but must plan such events and coordinate with other elements of the IADS.

The limited use of strike aircraft has increased the importance of artillery in the Ukraine War. Both combatants have large and well-developed artillery forces, a legacy of both army's Soviet heritage. The largest problem has been acquiring sufficient supplies of ammunition. Projections of artillery ammunition expenditure in a major war proved to be low on both sides, and each has experienced 'shell hunger' at various times. In early 2024 this problem became acute for the Ukrainians when US assistance was delayed by Republican politicians in the US Congress sympathetic to Russia.

The cost of the war can only be measured in general terms as both sides and their supporters release extensive propaganda, making correct assessments impossible. One US Department of Defense estimate placed total Russian casualties at around 315,000 as of February 2024. Another US estimate puts total casualties on both sides at about 500,000, including perhaps 70,000 Ukrainian killed. Thousands of civilians have also been killed or wounded. Accurate numbers will not be available until after the war, if ever. Millions more have been displaced or forcibly moved.

Both sides are resiliently continuing the war, with no indications of an end in the near term. The war's outcome is anything but certain.

ABOVE: Russian soldiers of the 55th Motor Rifle Brigade in Adiivka in February 2024. The city was heavily damaged in the fighting. (RUSSIAN MOD)

LEFT: Details are scant on the activities of Special Operations Forces (SOF) on both sides in Ukraine. This Ukrainian SOF soldier carries a HS .50-calibre rifle during operations in July 2022. (UKRAINIAN MOD)

ORGANISATION

The Ukrainian Military

Evolving under fire

RIGHT: Ukrainian Special Operations Forces have made several successful raids into Crimea and elsewhere during this war. These operators are armed with Ukrainian-made Malyuk assault rifles. (US ARMY)

BELOW: The Ukrainian air force focus has been to preserve their aircraft and pilots, using them only on missions where the goals justify the risk, as aircraft like these SU-27s are irreplaceable. (UK MOD/CROWN COPYRIGHT)

The Ukrainian Army formed out of the remnants of the Red Army after the Soviet Union dissolved in 1991. Due to its location in Eastern Europe, substantial Soviet forces were stationed in Ukraine during the Cold War including ground, naval and air forces along with nuclear weapons. This included almost 800,000 personnel, approximately 13,000 tanks and armoured vehicles, over 1,000 combat aircraft and hundreds of naval vessels. The Soviets stationed about 5,000 nuclear warheads in Ukraine, but these were all removed to Russia as part of a 1994 treaty.

Ukraine lacked the finances to support such a large conventional force, so many of the weapons were placed into storage or sold and the military shrunk to a more manageable size. Many in Ukraine feared becoming a Russian vassal state and so attempts were made to rebuild the military and create an indigenous arms industry, using the remnants of the Soviet facilities. These efforts met with both successes and challenges; a few units were combat ready but shortages of modern equipment and problems with corruption remained. Ukraine also began gradually integrating with the West and a hoped-for membership in NATO.

When Russia seized Crimea and the War in Donbass began in 2014, the Ukrainian army was unprepared and much of the initial fighting fell on National Guard and Territorial Defence units, which were officially part of the Ministry of internal Affairs. Over time the Ukrainian military forces improved, the result of a series of reforms impelled by the reality of the war.

In the years since, the Donbass fighting lessened into a simmering border conflict and Ukraine continued to work with Western militaries to improve its forces. In particular, Ukraine has worked to shed its Soviet-era command and staff organisation in favour of a more Western-style leadership model. Efforts were also made to integrate the reserves, National Guard and Territorial Defence Forces into the total Ukrainian military.

On the eve of the February 2022 Russian invasion, the Ukrainian military fell under the General Staff as its overall command. The General Staff controls the separate Land, Air and Naval Forces, the Special Operations Forces, Airborne Assault Forces and the Joint Forces Command, which oversaw the lines in Luhansk and Donetsk. It also oversees support functions such as medical, logistics, signals and cyber troops.

The Land Forces controlled the active brigades, which were generally staffed at 30 – 60 percent of full strength, to be completed by mobilised reservists

Estimated Ukrainian Army Strength, February 2022 (Prewar)

Under Central Command	Airborne Assault Command
15th Rocket Artillery Regiment	25th Airborne Brigade "Sicheslavska"
19th Rocket Artillery Brigade "Saint Barbara"	45th Air Assault Brigade
107th Rocket Artillery Regiment	46th Air Assault Brigade
27th Rocket Artillery Brigade "Sumy"	79th Air Assault Brigade
43rd Artillery Brigade "Hetman Taras Tryasyl"	81st Air Assault Brigade
	95th Air Assault Brigade

OK North (HQ Chernihiv)	OK South (HQ Odessa)
1st Operational Brigade National Guard	18th Special Operations Regiment "Azov" National Guard
4th Rapid Reaction Brigade National Guard	28th Mechanised Brigade
1st Tank Brigade "Severia"	32nd Naval Rocket Artillery Brigade
26th Artillery Brigade	36th Naval Infantry Brigade "Rear Admiral Mikhail Bilinsky"
30th Mechanised Brigade "Prince Konstantyn Ostrogski"	56th Motorised Infantry Brigade
58th Motorised Infantry Brigade	57th Motorised Infantry Brigade "Kostya Gordienko"
72nd Mechanised Brigade "Chornych Zaporozhtsiv"	59th Motorised Infantry Brigade "Yakov Gandziuk"
16th Independent Army Aviation Brigade	40th Artillery Brigade "Grand Duke Vytautas"
1129th Anti-Aircraft Regiment	11th Independent Army Aviation Brigade
1139th Anti-Aircraft Missile Regiment	38th Anti-Aircraft Missile Regiment
61st Jaeger Brigade	5 Territorial Defence Brigades (120th – 124th)
7 Territorial Defence Brigades (112th, 114th – 119th)	

OK East (HQ Dnipro)	OK West (HQ Rivne)
3rd Operational Brigade National Guard	2nd Operational Brigade National Guard
17th Tank Brigade "Konstantin Pestushko"	80th Air Assault Brigade
35th Naval Infantry Brigade	10th Mountain Assault Brigade
53rd Mechanised Brigade "Prince Vladimir Monomakh"	128th Mountain Assault Brigade "Zakarpattia"
54th Mechanised Brigade	14th Mechanised Brigade "Prince Roman the Great"
55th Artillery Brigade "Zaporizhian Sich"	24th Mechanised Brigade "King Daniel of Galicia"
92nd Mechanised Brigade "Ivan Sirko"	44th Artillery Brigade
93rd Mechanised Brigade "Kholodny Yar"	12th Independent Army Aviation Brigade
18th Independent Army Aviation Brigade	10th Naval Aviation Brigade
1039th Anti-Aircraft Missile Regiment	39th Anti-Aircraft Missile Regiment
5 Territorial Defence Brigades (108th – 111th, 113th)	8 Territorial Defence Brigades (100th – 107th)

Reserve Corps (many at cadre strength)	Total force:
3rd Tank Brigade	7 Airborne/Air Assault Brigades
4th Tank Brigade	5 Tank brigades
5th Tank Brigade	9 Mechanised Brigades
60th Mechanised Brigade	4 Motorised Infantry Brigades
62nd Mechanised Brigade	1 Jaeger Brigade
63rd Mechanised Brigade	2 Mountain Infantry Brigades
66th Mechanised Brigade	7 Artillery Brigades
38th Artillery Brigade	5 Rocket Artillery Brigades/Regiments
45th Artillery Brigade	5 Anti-Aircraft Regiments
	5 Aviation Brigades
	25 Territorial Defence Brigades
	5 National Guard Brigades
	2 Naval Infantry Brigades

Notes: New units have been raised since the February 2022 and some units have been reassigned to different OKs.

ORGANISATION

RIGHT: Maintenance is vital for modern armies. This mobile repair station was purchased by the Come Back Alive non-profit organisation. (UKRAINIAN MOD)

BELOW: Like the Ukrainian Air Force, the Navy is badly outnumbered and must husband its forces for critical operations. It can conduct riverine operations using its landing craft and smaller gunboats. (UKRAINIAN JOINT FORCES COMMAND)

in the event of war. Each brigade is issued up to 90 percent of its weapons and equipment. Artillery brigades usually have a battalion of motorised infantry for security. A Reserve Corps oversees nine tank, infantry and artillery brigades; prewar they were at a cadre strength of 5 – 10 percent and generally lacked heavy weaponry.

The Ukrainian army is organised into brigades and does not have divisions or corps. Rather, the Land Forces are organised into four regional commands, North, South, East and West. Each is assigned brigades and also oversees any Territorial Defence Brigades within its region. At the beginning of the war the Territorial Brigades were still being organised and were staffed, armed and equipped at varying levels of readiness.

Combat brigade composition depends on unit type. Infantry brigades generally have three infantry battalions and one tank battalion, while a tank brigade has three tank and one infantry battalion. Tank and mechanised brigades have an artillery group with four divisions, each the size of a Western battalion. Two divisions are equipped with 2S1 and 2S3 self-propelled guns, one with BM-21 Grad MLRS and the fourth is an anti-tank division with a dozen MT-12 Rapira anti-tank guns and nine Shturm-S tank destroyers, an MT-LB APC carrying ATGM. Brigades also have an air defence division and detachments of engineers, medical, reconnaissance, logistic and electronic warfare troops. Many brigades are now re-equipped with western weapons.

The Air Forces are also organised into brigades and regiments. It also oversees regional commands, named ACs North, South, West and Centre. Each had one or two brigades of combat aircraft and two to three air defence brigades or regiments. The Air Force also has several units of combat and support aircraft kept under central control. In general, the lighter air defence missile systems and MANPADS are controlled by the army while larger missiles systems such as the S-300, and later Patriot and NASAMs, are employed by the Air Force.

The Navy is small, with only a few patrol and missile craft along with some auxiliary ships. It does control a respectable force of shore based anti-ship missile systems, equipped with Neptune and Harpoon missiles. It also possesses a small number of Bayraktar UAS which have been used to good effect, especially early in the war during the fighting for Snake Island.

Overall, the Ukrainian military has performed much better than many expected before the 2022 war began. It has taken heavy casualties but remained able to keep the larger and better equipped Russian

WEAPONS OF THE UKRAINE WAR

military from making many gains since the initial invasion. Its first counteroffensive in the latter half of 2022 was very successful overall, while the 2023 offensive proved much less effective.

One growing criticism falls on Ukraine's brigade-centric organisation. Some brigades have struggled at times to put more than a few companies or a battalion into action at a time. Many critics urge Ukraine to reform their brigade and regional command structure into one with divisions and corps formed from the regional commands. Such a model would allow the brigades to be organised into divisions able to coordinate actions more effectively. Each region would become a corps with two or three divisions including Territorial Defence Brigades. The reserve would form a fifth corps of at least three divisions to provide the power needed for effective offensive action. This would be difficult to implement during active warfighting but could improve the results of future counteroffensives.

ABOVE: Since neither side can attain air superiority, artillery provides the primary fire support in this conflict. This Ukrainian 2S7 Pion belongs to the 43rd Artillery Brigade. The soldier is holding a card commemorating those lost at the Azovstal steel plant early in the war. (UKRAINIAN MOD)

LEFT: The Ukrainian military makes wide use of small trucks for transport and as armed 'technicals.' Though unarmoured, these fast vehicles can be used for casualty evacuation, raids or to respond quickly to threatened parts of the line in a mobile defence. (UKRAINIAN MOD)

ORGANISATION

The Russian Armed Forces

Successor to the Soviet military

Russia inherited the bulk of Soviet military forces in 1991. It had to remove the troops stationed in Eastern Europe, losing extensive basing facilities and then demobilised the bulk of its forces. The country's poor economy in the 1990s was inadequate to sustain large, advanced military forces; the troops who were left were often unpaid for months at a time and even lacked food. Many units were unable to do any military training at all. This parlous situation continued well into the 2000s.

While the Russian military was struggling to survive, it also had to take part in several regional conflicts, including actions in Moldova and Tajikistan, followed by Chechnya in 1994 - 2005. Chechnya showcased both the weakness of post-Soviet Russian forces and, over time, Russia's latent power and ability to keep fighting even after serious defeats.

The eventual success in Chechnya helped cement Vladimir Putin's ascendance to the Russian presidency.

Once in power, Putin began an effort to reform the Russian military through a series of defence ministers. These ministers, to greater or lesser degrees, attempted to curb corruption, improve efficiency and rationalise spending. The use of

RIGHT: MT-LB personnel carriers being refurbished at a factory in Tatarstan. Russia's large store of older armoured vehicles has provided a ready source of outdated but serviceable vehicles.
(RUSSIAN MOD)

BELOW: The corvette *Orekhovo-Zuyevo* of the Black Sea Fleet firing countermeasures during a prewar exercise.
(RUSSIAN MOD)

16 WEAPONS OF THE UKRAINE WAR

WEAPONS OF THE UKRAINE WAR

Estimated BTG Strength of Russian Forces in the Ukraine Operation, February 2022

Formation	BTGs	Formation	BTGs
35th Combined Arms Army		**6th Combined Arms Army**	
5th Guards Tank Brigade	2	25th Guards Motor Rifle Brigade	1
31st Guards Airborne Brigade	1	138th Guards Motor Rifle Brigade	2
36th Guards Motor Rifle Brigade	1	2nd Guards Motor Rifle Division	2
37th Guards Motor Rifle Brigade	2	144th Motor Rifle Division	6
38th Guards Motor Rifle Brigade	1	**20th Combined Arms Army**	
45th Guards Spetsnaz	1	3rd Motor Rifle Division	5
64th Motor Rifle Brigade	1	**II Army Corps (Luhansk)**	
69th Covering Brigade	1	4 brigades, 1 motor rifle regiment	*
76th Guards Airborne Division	2	1 artillery brigade	*
98th Guards Airborne Division	4	**I Army Corps (Donetsk)**	
106th Guards Airborne Division	4	5 brigades, 1 motor rifle regiment	*
41st Combined Arms Army		1 artillery brigade	*
35th Guards Motor Rifle Brigade	2	**8th Combined Arms Army**	
55th Motor Rifle Brigade	2	150th Motor Rifle Division	5-8
74th Guards Motor Rifle Brigade	2	**58th Combined Arms Army**	
90th Tank Division	4	7th Guards Airborne Division	4-6
2nd Guards Combined Arms Army		42nd Guards Motor Rifle Division	6
15th Guards Motor Rifle Brigade	1	136th Guards Motor Rifle Brigade	2
138th Guards Motor Rifle Brigade	1-2	336th Guards Naval Infantry Brigade	1
1st Guards Tank Army		**49th Combined Arms Army**	
27th Motor Rifle Brigade	3	19th Motor Rifle Division	3
200th Motor Rifle Brigade	2	20th Guards Motor Rifle Division	6
2nd Guards Motor Rifle Division	6	177th Naval Infantry Regiment	1-2
4th Guards Tank Division	8	810th Guards Naval Infantry Brigade	2
47th Guards Tank Division	5	**Total Estimated BTGs**	102-109

Notes: *The Luhansk and Donetsk Army Corps fielded up to 49 battalion equivalents in their tables of organisation but it is unknown how many took part in the initial offensive operations.

conscripts was reduced in favour of professional 'contract' soldiers and efforts to reduce the number of excess officers and professionalise the Non-Commissioned Officer (NCO) ranks took place. New weapons and equipment were adopted.

These efforts were not entirely successful. The 2008 War with Georgia, Russian support of Syria and of the Luhansk and Donetsk separatists showed that while Russia was able to engage in limited wars, it still lacked the ability to engage a peer opponent in a conventional conflict. Corruption was still an issue, as was the lack of professionalisation of troops and the difficulty in acquiring adequate numbers of new weapons and equipment. Success in the aforementioned conflicts masked some of these shortfalls.

The Russian General Staff exercises operational command through four Operational Strategic Commands (OSK), each covering a region of the country: Western, Southern, Central and Eastern. An OSK controls all land, air and naval forces within its assigned territory. This does not include the Strategic Forces, Special Forces, or Airborne Assault Troops (VDV), which remain under central control by the Defence Ministry.

For a period in the 2010s Russia reformed its army into

BELOW: A modern army stays on the move thanks to its fuel tankers. Even the most powerful armoured column grinds to a halt without them. (RUSSIAN MOD)

ORGANISATION

ABOVE: Russian paratroopers pose with captured Ukrainian weapons, including Javelins, NLAWs and MANPADS. Such seizures will be studied and tested to develop countermeasures. (RUSSIAN MOD)

BELOW: A Russian T-72 tank crosses an assault bridge in Ukraine. Rivers are major obstacles in warfare and bridging them usually draws enemy attention. (RUSSIAN MOD)

a brigade-centric organisation, reorganising each division into one or more brigades. These brigades have a mix of contract soldiers and conscripts. Partly due to personnel shortages and also out of a political need to prevent conscripts from deploying into combat and becoming casualties, brigades formed ad hoc Battalion Tactical Groups (BTGs). These are often composed of a few companies of tanks and infantry with supporting artillery, air defence and engineer elements.

However, experience fighting in the Donbass showed BTGs were not large enough to support themselves in the field for extended periods. Even when victorious in combat they often could not follow up their success. This eventually led to the recreation of divisions which could organise under field armies and provide support to their subordinate brigades and BTGs. This process remained incomplete when the current war began. For the 2022 Invasion of Ukraine, each division or brigade fielded one or more BTGs.

Each division oversees two or three combat brigades with supporting artillery, air defence and logistics units. Artillery units tend to be robust in the Russian Army, which has long prized the firepower of artillery. Battlefield ballistic missiles with conventional warheads are also used frequently. For the Ukraine operation the army was bolstered by units from the Border Guard Service, Rosgvardia (National Guard), OMON (Mobile Special Purpose Detachments) and police units. Chechen units which have served in Ukraine are part of the Rosgvardia.

Russia also uses private military companies, the most famous of which is the Wagner Group under the now-deceased Yevgeny Prigozhin. The group is largely defunct since he orchestrated a revolt against the Russian government. Wagner famously employed large numbers of troops recruited from Russian prisons to bolster its numbers, though the army also did so.

The Russian Aerospace Forces oversee the Air Force, Space Troops and Air Defence and Missile Troops. Combat aircraft are organised into regiments; fighter regiments usually have two or three squadrons with 8 – 12 aircraft each, while helicopter regiments have two or three squadrons of 12-16 aircraft each. One squadron is equipped with attack helicopters while the other two have transport or cargo models. Most Russian combat aircraft are modernised versions of Soviet-era types.

The Black Sea Fleet is Russia's naval force in the Ukraine War. After the seizure of Crimea in 2014, it was substantially rebuilt, receiving large numbers of new ships, air defence missiles and aircraft. Many of its ships can launch cruise missiles from vertical launch tubes and these are used as part of the Russian

WEAPONS OF THE UKRAINE WAR

LEFT: Russia has extensive air defences in place around Ukraine, such as this S-400 system. This advanced weapon can also be used in a ground attack mode.
(RUSSIAN MOD)

missile offensive against Ukrainian infrastructure. It also possesses a substantial force of amphibious warfare ships.

When the invasion began in February 2022, many observers expected the Russian military to achieve a quick victory. When the operation failed to achieve victory, it exposed problems at numerous levels, including training, maintenance, logistics, leadership and planning. For example, shortages of trained infantry plagued many units and shortages of precision munitions meant close air support missions used unguided bombs and rockets and placed aircraft in range of Ukrainian air defences. In 2022, Ukraine was able to stop the Russian offensive and launch a successful counteroffensive, leading observer to decry the Russian military's capabilities.

However, it is also apparent the Russian military has improved from 2023 onward. They have created effective defensive works and supported them adequately to prevent Ukrainian success in its 2023 offensive. It has used its latent power to refurbish dated but numerous weapons from storage to maintain battlefield strength and a February 2024 report from the UK's International Institute for Strategic Studies indicates the Russians can continue to restore older armoured vehicles for two to three more years before running out of inventory.

The Russian military has shown the ability to improvise on the battlefield and absorb lessons. Notably, this makes Russia one of the few countries with actual warfighting experience against a peer opponent.

BELOW: A Russian Su-34 landing at Buturlinovka Air Base. Note the drag parachute deploying and several unexpended bombs still on its ordnance pylons.
(RUSSIAN MOD)

www.keymilitary.com **19**

SMALL ARMS

AK-74

The standard rifle of both armies

RIGHT: The AK-74 is more controllable in full-automatic fire than its predecessor, the AKM. The lighter 5.45mm round allows the soldier to carry more ammunition than possible with the AKM as well. (UKRAINIAN MOD)

BELOW: Three of these Russian mechanised infantry have GP underbarrel grenade launchers attached to their rifles. The launcher can be sited out to 400 meters (1,312 feet). (RUSSIAN MOD)

While there are many different types of small arms in use in Ukraine, the AK-74 is the standard issue rifle for both the Russian and Ukrainian ground forces. Ukraine issues the standard AK-74, while the Russian use the AK-74M, a modernised version introduced in 1991 with various improvements for both service use and manufacturing. The Russians also produce the Universal Upgrade Kit (UUK), which includes a new dust cover, safety, vertical foregrip and rails for mounting optical sights, laser sights and lighting systems.

The AK-74 entered service in 1974 and is a development of the Kalashnikov AK-47/AKM series of rifles. During the late Cold War, many nations were transitioning to smaller, higher velocity cartridges for infantry rifles and the AK-74 was, in simple terms, an AKM chambered for the then-new Soviet 5.45mm round.

20 WEAPONS OF THE UKRAINE WAR

WEAPONS OF THE UKRAINE WAR

AK-74 Specifications	
Production	1974 - present
Caliber	5.45x39mm
Velocity	880m/s (2,900ft/s)
Magazine	30-round box magazine standard; weapon can use 45, 60 or 96 round magazines from the RPK-74 series machine guns
Weight	AK-74: 3.07kg (6.8lbs) AK-74M: 3.4kg (7.5lbs)
Maximum effective range	500m (1,650ft)
Rate of Fire	650 rounds per minute
Length	94.3cm (37.1 inches)

The weapon soon became standard issue for the Warsaw Pact and is widely used among the former states of the Soviet Union. It saw combat in Afghanistan, Chechnya, Georgia and elsewhere before the Ukraine War.

The Russians also issue the AK-12, a further modernised version of the AK-74M, adopted in 2018. It tends to be used by elite troops as the rifle was developed alongside the Russian Ratnik program, which introduced a series of new equipment for Russian troops but is not yet universally issued. The rifle is made by the Kalashnikov Concern, formerly Izhmash. The Russian government also requested a version firing the 7.62x39mm cartridge used by the AKM, likely due to the widespread use of that cartridge within Russia. That weapon is known as the AK-15, and its stated use is by special operations forces, who may sometimes prefer the larger, heavier 7.62mm round.

AK-74s are frequently seen with the GP series of 40mm underbarrel grenade launchers, which can fire fragmentation or smoke rounds. Both armies use these weapons as well.

Some AK-74Ms and AK-12s were captured by Ukrainian troops and have been put to use due to their familiarity and common ammunition. All these weapons are essentially derived from the AKM and have similar operating procedures for loading/unloading, firing, field stripping and cleaning. The Ukrainians do not manufacture the AK-74 but with so many on hand, it will be a mainstay of their forces for years to some.

ABOVE LEFT: This member of Ukraine's 10th Territorial Defence Brigade of Zaporizhzhia is carrying a captured Russian AK-12. He's using the 45-round magazine from an RPK-74 light machine gun. (UKRAINIAN MOD)

LEFT: This well-equipped Russian Soldier is carrying a very new-looking AK-15 rifle. Note the magazine has small clear plastic windows with round counts next to them so the user can track ammunition usage. (RUSSIAN MOD)

LEFT: This older image of a Russian naval infantryman shows an AKS-74 with a side-folding metal stock, designed for use by paratroopers, air assault and other elite troops. (US NAVY)

www.keymilitary.com 21

SMALL ARMS

Light and General-Purpose Machine Guns

Portable firepower for the infantry

ABOVE: A soldier of the Russian 247th Guards Air Assault Regiment mans a PKP Pecheneg GPMG. Note the sight mounted on the weapon, visible just past the soldier's helmet. (RUSSIAN MOD)

RIGHT: A Ukrainian soldier crouching behind a BMP infantry fighting vehicle with his RPK light machine gun. This old but effective weapon is in second-line service throughout Ukraine. (US ARMY)

Though they are also widely mounted on vehicles of all types, machine guns are what provide infantry units the firepower to attack, defend and manoeuvre on the battlefield. As with other weapon types in this conflict, the Ukrainian and Russian forces mostly use the same weapon types, all of them either Soviet-era or updated versions of Soviet designs. Additionally, the Ukrainians have over a dozen Western models which have been donated by NATO nations or purchased abroad.

The oldest machine gun in widespread use is the PM1910, based on the Maxim gun of the early 20th Century. It saw service throughout both world wars and afterward; in Ukraine they have seen use since the Crimean invasion and Donbass War of 2014. This water-cooled

22 WEAPONS OF THE UKRAINE WAR

WEAPONS OF THE UKRAINE WAR

Specifications of Major Machine Gun Types						
Weapon	PM1910	RPK	RPK-74	PK	MG-3	FN MAG
Origin	Russia	Soviet Union	Soviet Union	Soviet Union	Germany	Belgium
Caliber	7.62x54R	7.62x39mm	5.45x39mm	7.62x54R	7.62x51mm NATO	7.62x51mm NATO
Feed	250-rd belt	30, 40 or 75 rd magazine	30 or 45rd magazine	50 to 250rd belts	50-100rd belt	100rd belt
Weight	62.66kg	4.8kg	4.7kg	9kg	11.5kg	11.8kg
Rate of fire*	600	600	600	800	800-1,200	650-1,000
Effective range	2,700m	1,000m	1,000m	1,000m	1,200m	1,800m

* In rounds per minute

weapon is typically mounted on a compact wheeled carriage with a small gun shield. The Ukrainians use them primarily in fixed defensive positions though they have been seen on vehicles. When asked in 2016 why Ukraine still employed them, then-Chief of the General Staff Victor Muzhenko replied "On stationary posts… they perform perfectly. Moreover, we have over 30,000 of them in our stores."

At the squad level the RPK is a common sight. The RPK is visually similar to the AK-series of rifles but with a longer barrel and some other modifications to make it capable of sustained firing. RPKs are most often seen in the Ukrainian National Guard. The RPK-74, which fires the same ammunition as the AK-74, is the standard issue Light Machine Gun (LMG) army-wide when it is available. For the Russians, the RPK-74M (for 'modernised') is the standard issue light machine gun and is also usually seen at the squad level.

The next step up is the General-Purpose Machine Gun (GPMG), almost always a belt-fed weapon and issued either at the platoon level or to specialised weapons platoons within companies and battalions. For both armies the PKM machine gun is standard issue, though the Russian have introduced an updated version called the PKP Pecheneg. This new weapon has an improved barrel cooling system and is more accurate. It also has a rail system to mount optical sights or night vision devices. The Pecheneg is gradually replacing the PKM.

All these weapons are considered effective, durable and reliable, though the RPKs must be reloaded more often due to the limited capacity their fixed magazines. Their common Soviet-origin ammunition also eases logistical constraints, as even captured ammunition can be used.

The Western machine guns in Ukrainian service are mostly GPMGs such as the FN MAG (known in the UK as the L7 and USA as the M240) and German MG 3, an updated version of the WWII-era MG 42. MG 3 variants have been donated by Germany and Italy and an old Yugoslavian version has been seen in Ukraine as well. These are also effective weapons as long as ammunition can be obtained for them.

LEFT: The PKM soldiers on as Ukraine's standard GPMG. The soldier's lack of kit shows he is likely on exercise. Note the empty rail mount for an optical sight just above the weapon's receiver. (US ARMY)

LEFT: Scouts from the Ukrainian 3rd Tank Brigade with a captured PKP Pecheneg machine gun. Though festooned with rifles and antitank weapons, they carry little personal kit so they can move quickly. (UKRAINIAN MOD)

BELOW: This Ukrainian scout has an ad hoc sidecar for his motorcycle mounting an MG42/59, a licensed copy of the German MG 3, produced in Italy by Beretta. The Italian version has a heavier bolt, slowing the rate of fire to 800 rounds per minute. (UKRAINIAN MOD)

SMALL ARMS

Heavy Machine Guns
Firepower and versatility

RIGHT: A Polish trainer instructs Ukrainian troops on the use of the DSHK HMG. The improvised bipod mount allows the crew to stay lower to the ground and less vulnerable to incoming fire. (US ARMY)

While GPMGs fire rifle-calibre cartridges in the 7.62mm range, Heavy Machine Guns (HMGs) are distinguished by their larger calibre, in the 12-14mm range. They are also of larger size and weight to handle the recoil and power of their more massive ammunition. This also gives them effective hitting power at longer ranges, usually out to 2,000 meters of more.

HMGs are among the most versatile weapons in military service. They are useful against personnel, aircraft, Unmanned Aerial Systems (UAS), unarmoured and lightly armoured vehicles, boats and small ships, as well as being able to penetrate light fortifications. When being trained on the .50-calibre Browning M2, the author recalls being told it would reliably penetrate the side armour of a BMP fighting vehicle at less than 400 meters.

RIGHT: The DSHK fires a large 12.7mm cartridge equivalent to the Western .50-caliber round. This powerful round is very effective against unarmoured or lightly armoured vehicles as well. (US ARMY)

These machine guns are ground mounted for infantry use, used on tanks and armoured fighting vehicles, used to arm helicopters and occasionally aircraft. They are also used as anti-aircraft weapons, often with their own special mounts to allow firing at high angles. HMGs are frequently used on naval vessels as they are effective against small vessels such as fast attack craft and suicide boats. Even small ships are vulnerable to their penetration capabilities.

In Ukraine, HMGs are widely issued and prized for this versatility. A commander of a Ukrainian machine gun unit, call sign 'Fanat,' stated, "These heavy machine guns will bolster our capabilities in neutralising enemy infantry and Russian light armoured vehicles from distances up to 800 meters. Also, they will aid in targeting low-flying aircraft, as well as suppressing enemy fire points and strongholds."

There are four main types of HMG in service in Ukraine. Two are in use with both armies, one is solely Russian and the other sold or given to Ukraine as military aid. All are belt-fed weapons, with ammunition belts normally in the 50 to 100 round range due to the large size of the cartridges.

RIGHT: The muzzle blast of the DSHK is considerable and can blind the firer as well as reveal their position. Note the large muzzle brake on a neighbouring weapon at upper right; it serves to reduce recoil. (US ARMY)

DSHK 1938: Designed by the Soviets shortly before World War II, this long-serving weapon is nicknamed the 'Dushka.' It has seen combat use around the globe and is often mounted on armoured vehicles of all types. The Ukrainians have modified many of their DShKs with a bipod and shoulder stock to allow them to be used in trenches and fortifications. This version has a large muzzle brake

24 WEAPONS OF THE UKRAINE WAR

WEAPONS OF THE UKRAINE WAR

ABOVE: A Russian paratrooper operates his NSV HMG from atop an armoured vehicle in March 2022. It fires the same cartridge as the DShK. (RUSSIAN MOD)

Primary Heavy Machine Guns used in Ukraine				
Weapon	DShK 1938	NSV	Kord	Browning M2
Origin	Soviet Union	Soviet Union	Russia	United States
Caliber	12.7x108mm	12.7x108mm	12.7x108mm	12.7x99mm
Weight*	34kg (75lb)	25kg (55.1 lb)	32kg (71lb)**	38kg (84lb)
Rate of Fire***	600	700-800	600-650	450-600
Effective Range	2,000m	2,000m	2,000m	1,800m

* Weapon only without mount (ex: tripod) or ammunition
** Infantry version with bipod
*** In rounds per minute

added to help control the heavy recoil and a modified trigger mechanism to replace the standard butterfly triggers actuated with the thumbs.

NSV: Intended as a replacement for the DShK, this Soviet design entered service in 1971. It has been copied by Ukraine and several other nations. It has also seen service worldwide. Ukrainian Territorial Defence units often mount them in technicals such as the ubiquitous Toyota pickup. The NSV is the standard HMG of the Russian Army.

Kord: Entering service in 1998, the Kord is intended as the replacement for the NSV. It is gradually replacing that weapon. Externally similar to the NSV, the Kord has a new bolt and gas system and a new muzzle brake. It is lighter than previous Soviet-era models, making it easier for a two-soldier machine gun team to move.

Browning M2: Known affectionately as the 'Ma Deuce,' or simply the "fifty-cal," this is the standard HMG in the West. The Ukrainians received many as military aid, including over 600 of the Turkish license-built version, the CANiK M2.

Some Ukrainians prize the M2 over its Soviet-designed counterparts. 'Vasyl,' a Ukrainian machine gunner who served near Bakhmut, has used DShKs, NSVs and M2s. He preferred the M2. "It's much better because it doesn't fail," he said. "When you fire a Soviet one it often gets jammed after a few shots just because of the dust getting in. With the Browning, even when it jams, you jerk it [referring to the charging handle] and keeps working. No problem."

BELOW: A Ukrainian soldier of the 46th Air Assault Brigade firing a Browning M2 50-caliber HMG in May 2022. It is the only Western HMG in service in the conflict. (UKRAINIAN MOD)

www.keymilitary.com 25

SMALL ARMS

Other Small Arms

From Cold War hand-me-downs to the latest production

The Ukraine War revealed to the world how quickly the modern battlefield uses up not only munitions, but the weapons which use them. Both Russia and Ukraine have vastly expanded the size of their militaries, requiring small arms from pistols to machine guns to equip their larger forces. Small arms are also routinely damaged, lost or captured in combat, requiring replacement.

Many of these small arms come from Soviet-era stockpiles. The Soviet Union was known to place surplus weapons into storage, retaining them long after they became obsolete. Both Russia and Ukraine inherited such stockpiles after the Soviet Union collapsed in 1991. Millions of small arms were sold, not always legally, in the following years, but millions more remained. Not all of these surplus weapons were useful, as they often included arms from the Great War and World War II, and occasionally even old cavalry sabres and bayonets.

In May 2023 news reports appeared stating Russian Wagner mercenaries captured a salt mine near Soledar, Ukraine, formerly a Soviet storage depot. The late Evgeni Prigozhin, then head of Wagner, stated there were enough weapons in the mine to arm a million people, mostly composed of World War II-era submachine guns such as American-made Thompsons and Soviet PPSh-41

RIGHT: A Ukrainian marksman using a 'Dragunov' SVD rifle, a Soviet-era weapon which was issued at the platoon level in the Soviet Army. It remains in widespread use in both armies.
(US ARMY)

RIGHT: The AKM is likely the most common rifle in Ukraine after the AK-74. This member of the Ukrainian 79 Airmobile Brigade is exiting a BTR personnel carrier.
(US ARMY)

BELOW: A Ukrainian soldier of the 59th Motorised Brigade practices with a modern Polish-built FS Grot assault rifle. Ten thousand of these weapons were given to Ukraine by Poland and more have been ordered.
(UKRAINIAN MOD)

and PPS-43s. Most of the weapons were still in their original packing crates. It appeared the Ukrainian army had already moved most of the non-obsolete weapons.

Photographic evidence frequently appears online of various World War II weapons in use by soldiers in Ukraine, including the Thompson, PPSH-41, the German MG42 and the Model 1910 Maxim machine gun. How many of these weapons are officially issued rather than taken up by units in action on an ad hoc basis is unclear.

While the AK-74 is the standard-issue rifle for both nations, each has large numbers of older AKM rifles which are widely used. Both countries also issue specialised weapons to elite troops and special operations forces.

WEAPONS OF THE UKRAINE WAR

Ukraine received tens of thousands of small arms from various nations as military aid. This includes surplus Cold War weapons and new production, mostly from NATO members. In October 2023, the US Government announced it would send Ukraine thousands of Iranian small arms and over a million rounds of ammunition, originally intended for Houthi rebels in Yemen but confiscated by the US Navy.

FAR LEFT: The Malyuk rifle is made in Ukraine and is seen here in the hands of a Ukrainian marine during training with the UK Royal Navy. The rifle has some similarities to the Kalashnikov such as the selector lever and common magazine. (UK MOD/CROWN COPYRIGHT)

LEFT: This member of the Ukrainian International Legion is holding a captured ASM Val, a Soviet/Russian rifle with an integral suppressor and firing a subsonic 9x39mm cartridge from a 30-round magazine. It is typically used by special operations forces and reconnaissance troops. (UKRAINIAN MOD)

LEFT: The American M21 rifle is an accurised version of the 1960's M14 battle rifle, issued to snipers. It fires the standard 7.62 NATO round. This example is in use by a member of a Ukrainian Territorial Defence unit. (UKRAINIAN MOD)

BELOW: A Ukrainian marine sets up a German MG3 machine gun as his comrades exit a UK-supplied Mastiff MRAP. The MG3 is a Cold War version of the World War II MG42. This is likely an exercise as the gunner does not appear to have any ammunition at the ready for his weapon. (UKRAINIAN MOD)

www.keymilitary.com 27

ANTI-TANK WEAPONS

Stugna-P

Ukraine's Homemade ATGM

RIGHT: The Stugna-P is mounted on a tripod for ground firing. Note the remote-control unit and long cable to allow remote control.
(UKRAINIAN MOD)

In the early 2010s Ukraine began seeking replacements for its Soviet-era Anti-Tank Guided Missiles (ATGM). Ukrainian defence company Luchs Design Bureau, itself a descendant of the Soviet weapons industry, developed the Stugna-P, also known as the Stuhna-P or Skif in its export version.

The Stugna-P missiles come in two sizes, 130mm and 152mm. Each size is available with either a tandem-charge High Explosive Ant-Tank (HEAT) or a high-explosive fragmentation warhead. The launcher can use any of the four types of missile without modification. The launcher is controlled by a PDU-215 control console which connects to the launcher via a 50-meter-long cable, allowing the firer to use the weapon from a distance.

The tandem-charge warhead allows the Stugna-P to engage armoured vehicles equipped with explosive reactive armour (ERA). Tandem warheads have a first charge which either detonates or penetrates the ERA, preventing it from functioning properly, allowing the second charge to penetrate the vehicle's main armour.

Stugna-P is a laser beam-riding weapon. Typical laser guidance involves pointing a laser beam at the target, allowing the missile to home in on whatever the laser is hitting. Beam riding means the laser is pointed at the missile itself, which has a small port at the rear which detects the laser's coded pulses and alters its flight according to that input. This means the laser is not pointed at the target vehicle, which will not detect the laser even if it has a laser detection defence system. The weapon also has an overflight mode where it will fly above the target and dive onto it just before impact.

Ukrainian troops value the Stugna-P for its long range and remote-control capability. It has proven very effective against Russian armour. There are even two documented cases of the weapon shooting down Ka-52 attack helicopters. It can be mounted on BTR personnel carriers, lorries or fired from the ground. There is a thermal imager sight for the weapon, but most Ukrainian units do not have them due to their high cost.

Stugna-P ATGM		
Version	130mm	152mm
Missile Weight	30kg (66 lb)	37kg (82lb)
Full System Weight	97kg (214 lb)	104kg (229lb)
Range day	100- 5,000m (109-5470yds)	100-5,500m (109- 6010yds)
Range night	100-3,000m (109- 3280yds)	100-3,000m (109- 3280yds)
Armour penetration	1000mm (39in)	1,200mm (47in)

BELOW: A three-soldier crew normally operates the Stugna-P. This team in winter camouflage is carrying over 200lbs in addition to their personal kit and AK-74 rifles.
(UKRAINIAN MOD)

28 WEAPONS OF THE UKRAINE WAR

WEAPONS OF THE UKRAINE WAR

Javelin

Hard-hitting anti-tank firepower

MGM-148 Javelin ATGM	
Origin	United States
Missile Weight	15.9kg (35lb)
Full System Weight	22.3kg (49lb)
Range	65 to 4,000m
Warhead	Tandem Shaped Charge
Armour penetration	800mm (31.5in) of RHA

The Javelin is a battle-tested, effective anti-tank weapon whose reputation has been burnished on the battlefields of Ukraine. This American design entered service as the replacement for the Cold War M47 Dragon missile. Ukrainian forces have used the Javelin to destroy hundreds, if not thousands, of Russian tanks and armoured vehicles.

Unlike many antitank missiles which require wire guidance or an operator to steer the weapon into target, the Javelin is "fire and forget." The operator uses the Command Launch Unit (CLU) to lock the missile onto its target, after which the missile guides itself without further input by the firer. This allows the user to immediately move after firing to avoid return fire. The Javelin comes in a self-contained launch tube to which the user attaches the CLU. After firing, the tube is discarded and the CLU attached to the next tube for firing. Ukrainian troops often use the empty containers to build beds and other furnishing in the field.

The missile can be used for direct attack against buildings and bunkers for maximum penetration and blast effects against those kinds of targets. For strikes against armoured vehicles or certain types of fixed defences, the missile uses a top attack mode to penetrate the thinner top armour. The tandem warhead design has an initial charge to detonate any explosive reactive armour (ERA) so the main charge can penetrate the primary armour. Javelin can also engage low flying helicopters and has reportedly done so in Ukraine.

In the initial Russian invasion in February 2022, Javelins and other weapons were used against the large Russian columns in hit and run attacks along their flanks. Since then, they use drones to seek out Russian armour and sneak into range with Javelins for a surprise strike. The weapons were so valued in the beginning of the conflict a drawing depicting an orthodox-style religious figure cradling a Javelin launcher, named "Saint Javelin," became an internet meme and symbol of Ukrainian resistance. 'Javelin' and 'Javelina' are now popular names for pets and Ukrainian stores sell plush Javelin toys for children.

LEFT: The Russian Army occasionally captures Javelins, publicly stating the missiles are handed over to troops from the Donetsk and Luhansk regions, allied with the Russians in this war. (RUSSIAN MOD)

BELOW: A Ukrainian soldier of the 36th Brigade aims a Javelin using the CLU. Upon firing, the missile is ejected from the launch tube in a 'soft launch,' then the rocket motor ignites a safer distance from the firer. (UKRAINIAN MOD)

www.keymilitary.com 29

ANTI-TANK WEAPONS

NLAW

Fire and forget missile

RIGHT: The NLAW is quick to put into action, using a simple optical sight. Targets can be engaged within seconds. (UKRAINIAN MOD)

The Next-Generation Light Anti-Tank Weapon (NLAW) is a handheld shoulder-fired missile, provided to Ukraine alongside the Javelin and other Western ATGM. It is a single-shot, disposable weapon effective against armoured vehicles and fortified positions. Compared to the Javelin, it is shorter ranged and has less amour penetration, but is lighter and can be easily fired from within buildings and defensive positions, making it very versatile. One report stated the Javelin excels at long range, while the NLAW is good for close-in fighting.

The weapon is simple to use. The firer uses a small, attached sighting unit to aim at the target, tracking it for two to three seconds. It is not necessary for the firer to know the precise range to the target, as NLAW uses a predicted line-of sight system; the sight's software uses the firer's aiming movement to calculate the flight path the missile will follow.

When fired, the missile is soft-launched from the tube, flying eight meters away from the firer before the rocket motor ignites. This reduces back blast, allowing

BELOW: This NLAW missile will fly a few more meters before igniting its rocket motor. The missile covers about 400 meters in two seconds and can track stationary and moving targets. (UKRAINIAN MOD)

NLAW ATGM	
Origin	United Kingdom/Sweden
Weight	12.5kg (28lb)
Effective Range	800m
Warhead	High Explosive Anti-Tank
Armour penetration	500mm (19.7in)

it to be fired within more confined spaces. The warhead has optical and magnetic sensors to determine its detonation point.

For attacks on armoured vehicles, NLAW uses a top-attack mode, flying one meter over the line of sight before diving on the target's thinner roof armour. The user can set the arming distance for the warhead to prevent it from detonating over a previously knocked out vehicle. It can also be used in a direct attack mode against vehicles or defensive positions such as bunkers.

The United Kingdom is a major provider of NLAWS to Ukraine, providing at least 5,000. Some analysts believe the weapon may be responsible for up to 30-40 percent of Russian tank losses. NLAW's light weight means Ukrainian anti-tank teams could easily carry them in rapid movements to outflank Russian tank columns. This was especially effective early in the war when the armour often kept to roads and lacked proper infantry support. One Ukrainian soldier was recorded standing in front of a destroyed Russian tank, stating "I want to say a big thank you to our British comrades helping us."

WEAPONS OF THE UKRAINE WAR

9M133 Kornet

Advanced Russian ATGM

The Kornet is one of Russia's most effective anti-tank weapons. It can be ground-mounted on a tripod or on vehicles in four missile arrangements, often with two of these quad launchers atop a vehicle such as a GAZ Tigr armoured car. Its long range and high armour penetration make it a threat to any tank the Ukrainian military operates. It first entered service in the Russian army in 1998.

The man-portable version can be carried and set up by two soldiers, though carrying spare missiles would be a burden or require extra help. The weapon can be set up and ready to fire in less than a minute. In flight, the weapon is guided by beam riding, similar to the Stugna-P (see page 30). Kornet is capable of top attacks against the thinner roof armour of a tank or fighting vehicle.

Highly effective against tanks and armoured vehicles, they can also be used against fortifications, troops and other defences. One version of the Kornet is equipped with a thermobaric warhead for targets other than armour. There is also a version of the launcher which can be mounted on ships.

The Russian Army has used this weapon widely in Ukraine. Some were used during the 2014 Russian operation in Crimea and distributed to separatists of the breakaway Donetsk and Luhansk regions. Remnants of the missiles were found among battlefield debris, including other Russian equipment. Since the Ukrainian military never operated the Kornet, this was presented as evidence of Russian involvement in the conflict.

During the 2022 invasion, Kornets were used by the airborne and air assault troops who seized the Antonov airport near Kyiv. The Ukrainians were able to capture an unknown number of the weapon, which they have put to use. In early 2023 there were several reports in media of the Russian supplementing their own supplies of the Kornet with an Iranian licensed-made copy, known as the Dahlavieh. This copy is distinguishable by a red stripe around the front end of the launch tube, a marking not used in Russian production.

9M133 Kornet-M/EM ATGM	
Origin	Russia
Weight	64kg (141lb) with tripod/control unit
Effective Range	8,000m
Warhead	Tandem High Explosive Anti-Tank
Armour penetration	Up to 1,300mm (51.2in)

LEFT: This Russian crew set up their Kornet system to guard a road approach near Antonov Airport in February 2022. Russian troops readily took the airport at the beginning of the war but were unable to hold it. (RUSSIAN MOD)

BELOW: The Kornet is a large, capable ATGM widely used by Russian forces and exported widely around the world. They are effective even against modern main battle tanks. (RUSSIAN MOD)

ANTI-TANK WEAPONS

MT-12 Rapira

Cold War anti-tank gun

The MT-12 Rapira is a Soviet-era anti-tank cannon which entered service in 1970. It is an improved version of the T-12, which entered Soviet Service in 1961. Both versions have been seen in the Ukraine War, in use by both sides. The weapon has a smoothbore barrel and was one of the first tank or anti-tank guns to use Armour-Piercing Fin-Stabilised Discarding Sabot (APFSDS) ammunition, now standard for such weapons.

The MT-12 can also fire a High-Explosive Anti-Tank (HEAT) round, which has good armour penetration but is easily defeated by reactive armour. It can also fire the 9M117 series of laser guided missiles, which requires a laser aiming device attached to the weapon. There is also a version of the MT-12 with a radar sighting device to allow firing at night or in low visibility such as fog. There is also a high explosive fragmentation round for use against infantry or unarmoured targets.

The Ukrainians possessed around 500 Rapiras when the war began, and they are widely issued to Territorial Defence units, who use them in both the anti-tank and artillery roles. While these weapons would have limited effects against Russian main battle tanks, they would be effective against other armoured vehicles such as infantry fighting vehicles. A few enterprising Ukrainians have mounted their Rapiras on MT-LB armoured vehicles, which are often used as tractors for the towed version. This appears to be a local conversion rather than a widespread production effort.

Since they are generally a towed weapon, MT-12s are most effective when emplaced in a defensive position which does not require frequent movement. Their ability to function as an artillery piece gives them a valuable flexibility. The Russians Army has been seen using them in both roles as well, though primarily in the indirect fire mode. Artillery losses on both sides have been high and the Rapira is a serviceable replacement.

RIGHT: A gun crew with their Rapira, towed by an MT-LB. Note the lengthy ammunition crates at the vehicle's rear; the weapon's 100mm rounds are unusually long to give them more space for propellant. (UKRAINIAN JOINT FORCES COMMAND)

BELOW: A well-worn Rapira in direct fire mode. The weapon can easily penetrate lightly armoured vehicles but has difficulty against main battle tanks such as the T-72 or T-90. (UKRAINIAN MOD)

MT-12 Rapira Anti-tank gun	
Origin	Soviet Union
Calibre	100mm
Weight	3,050kg (6720lb)
Elevation	-6 to +20 degrees
Rate of fire	6-14 rounds per minute
Direct Fire Range	3,000m
Indirect Fire Range	8,200m

WEAPONS OF THE UKRAINE WAR

Panzerfaust 3

German anti-tank rocket

The Panzerfaust 3, designed by German company Dynamit Nobel AG, serves as the German Army's infantry anti-tank rocket system. The German military formally adopted it in 1992 and since then hundreds of thousands of the rockets have been produced and the weapon has been adopted by at least 10 nations. At least 3,000 Panzerfaust rockets were transferred to Ukraine at the beginning of the war in 2022.

The weapon's name derives from the World War II weapon of the same name, which translates as "armoured fist." Development began in the mid-1970s and designers intended it to provide a weapon for German infantry to use against then-new Soviet tank designs such as the T-72 and T-80.

The rocket system initially used a HEAT warhead, but later production models introduced a tandem charge version to defeat reactive armour. The spike on the front of the warhead has a small explosive charge to detonate the reactive armour, allowing the main charge to penetrate the tank's main armour. Unlike many other systems, the Panzerfaust 3 produces very little back blast. The rear of the firing tube contains a plastic granulate which counteracts the force of the projectile's launch.

There is also an anti-bunker munition, named the 'Bunkerfaust,' which can penetrate up to 360mm of concrete. The weapon warheads have a maximum range of 920m after which the warhead self-destructs to prevent becoming unexploded ordnance. Panzerfaust 3s are best suited for close-in fighting since they are unguided after firing and produce little backblast, making them useful in urban and built-up areas.

Panzerfaust 3s have been seen in the hands of Ukrainian Territorial Defence Force troops and were used widely in the beginning months of the war. Their portability made them ideal for anti-tank hunter teams attacking enemy columns from the flanks in hit and run-style attacks.

LEFT: The Netherlands and Germany gave Ukraine thousands of Panzerfaust 3s at the beginning of the conflict. They proved an excellent close-range anti-tank weapon. (NETHERLANDS MOD)

BELOW: The Panzerfaust 3 has seen several upgrades to its warhead to keep it effective against modern armoured vehicles. The spike on the front of the munition enables it to defeat reactive armour. (US ARMY)

Panzerfaust 3 Anti-tank Rocket	
Origin	Germany
Weight	15.6kg (34.5lb) with tandem warhead
Effective Range	920m
Warhead	Tandem Hollow Charge
Armour Penetration	900mm (35in) RHA

ANTI-TANK WEAPONS

Rocket Propelled Grenades

Russia's long-serving rocket launchers

RIGHT: A Ukrainian soldier fires an RPG, whose rocket flash can be seen in the distance. (US ARMY)

RIGHT: Two soldiers of the 79th Air Assault Brigade prepare to fire RPG-22s. After firing the tubes are discarded and the troops immediately move to new firing positions. (US ARMY)

BELOW: A rifleman puts down covering fire as his fellow soldier fires an RPG-7. Note the ground behind the firer has been disturbed by the weapon's back blast. (US ARMY)

The Rocket Propelled Grenade (RPG) is one of the ubiquitous small arms of the last 50 years. These handheld anti-tank rocket launchers have served in most of the world's conflicts during that time, used by soldiers, insurgents and terrorists alike. They are simple, easy to produce, inexpensive and durable.

RPGs are widely used in the Ukraine War, providing on-hand firepower for infantry squaddies. They are the most common handheld anti-tank weapon on the battlefield, far outnumbering weapons provided by the West to Ukraine or either combatant's guided antitank systems.

Despite its age, the most common system used in Ukraine is the RPG-7, which entered service in 1961 and is still in production in various places around the world, including the United States, which produces an updated version called the Precision Shoulder-fired Rocket Launcher-1 (PSRL-1). This weapon was sold to the Ukrainian Army beginning in 2017.

The RPG-7 makes a distinctive 'bang-whoosh' sound when fired and has a maximum range of 920

34 WEAPONS OF THE UKRAINE WAR

WEAPONS OF THE UKRAINE WAR

Selected Rocket-Propelled Grenade systems used in the Ukraine War						
Type	RPG-7	RPG-18	RPG-22	RPG-26	RPG-32
Origin	Soviet Union	Soviet Union	Soviet Union	Soviet Union	Russia, Jordan
Reloadable	Yes	No	No	No	Yes
Weight	7kg (15.4lb)	2.6kg (5.7lb)	2.8kg (6.2lb)	2.9kg (6.4lb)	10kg (22lb)
Effective Range	330m	200m	200mm	250m	350m
Warhead	HEAT, Thermobaric, Fragmentation	HEAT	HEAT	HEAT, Thermobaric	HEAT, Thermobaric
Armour Penetration	Up to 750mm (30 in) RHA	300mm (11.8in) RHA	400mm (15.7in) RHA	440mm (17.3in) RHA	750mm (30 in) RHA

meters. At that distance the rocket self-destructs, which can spread shrapnel over the immediate area. Soldiers have been known to use the RPG-7 at maximum range to shower an area occupied by enemy troops. Most RPG warheads are standard High-Explosive Anti-Tank (HEAT), but there are antipersonnel and thermobaric rockets available.

There are also newer RPG designs in use, some of which are reloadable and others single-shot weapons which are thrown away once the rocket is fired, like the American Cold War-era M72 Light Antitank Weapon (LAW). Thousands of M72s were also transferred to Ukraine at the beginning of the 2022 Russian invasion, many from Canada, Norway and Denmark. They have been seen in use by the Ukrainian Foreign Legion.

The Russian Army trains to use their RPG teams in concert with other troops to form 'Leopard Hunters,' combining snipers who aim at the aiming and vision devices on enemy tanks while the RPG teams manoeuvre to hit the tank in its flanks. These groups can also include teams with ATGM. The Leopard Hunter moniker is a reference to Soviet anti-tank assets in World War II, which were often called 'Big Game Hunters' because several German tanks were named for large cats. The name also points toward the Leopard I and II tanks Germany and other nations are supplying to Ukraine.

The Russian training scheme exemplifies RPGs are most effective when used in groups. An American study of RPG attacks during the Vietnam War showed that about one in seven RPGs fired at US armoured vehicles resulted in a hit. Of the seven which hit their target, only another one of seven caused a casualty or serious damage. While RPGs have better warheads in the 21st Century, the study does show how hard it can be to obtain a good hit with such weapons in the stress of combat.

ABOVE: A Ukrainian recruit reloads his RPG-7 during training. Beneath his hand can be seen the weapon's pistol grip with trigger at the front and hammer cocking piece at the rear. (US ARMY)

LEFT: RPGs produce a significant amount of flash and back blast when fired. In combat an RPG team normally relocates immediately to avoid any return fire. (US ARMY)

BELOW: A Ukrainian soldier prepares to fire and RPG-22 during the 2014-15 war against Russian-backed separatists in Eastern Ukraine. The BRDM-2 scout car behind him flies a Ukrainian flag as an identification measure since that model served on both sides. (UKRAINIAN MOD)

ARMOURED FIGHTING VEHICLES

T-64

Ukrainian Workhorse

ABOVE: Muzzle blast kicks up a cloud of snow and dust in front of a T-64B of the 14 Mechanised Brigade. After firing tank crews often move to a new firing position. (US ARMY)

The T-64 is the standard tank of the Ukrainian forces. Soviet designers began work on the T-64 in the early 1960s, and it was designed and produced in the Soviet tank factory in what is now Kharkiv, Ukraine. For logistical reasons, many T-64s were issued to units based in Ukraine, to be near the production site.

When Ukraine became independent in 1991, it gained 2,340 T-64s, of which 1,574 were the T-64B. Ukraine also gained some T-72s and T-80s, but lacked the ability to maintain them and so they were placed into storage. This made the T-64 Ukraine's standard main battle tank practically by default. When the Donbas War started in 2014, the Ukrainian army had about 700 tanks in service and around 600 of these were T-64Bs. About 85 of the rest were the T-64BM Bulat, a Ukrainian-devised upgraded model.

Most of these T-64s were in a bad condition as the Ukrainian economy couldn't fund proper maintenance or repair. In particular, the tank's electronics often failed, most of the explosives in their reactive armour blocks were expired due to age and the engine's automatic fire extinguishers often did not work. Some tanks were lost due to these faults, but crews also noticed that when the reactive armour functioned properly, the T-64 fared well against the Soviet-era anti-tank weapons the Separatist forces employed.

The Separatists also used T-64s, many of which were captured from Ukrainian forces or taken from storage depots. As the fighting turned against the Separatists they began to receive arms from Russia, including T-64s. This aided Russia in its deception efforts, as it was difficult to prove the provided T-64s were not from Ukrainian stocks. It is estimated the Russians supplied about 70-80 T-64s in 2014. Afterward Russia began supplying T-72s as numbers of serviceable T-64s dwindled.

Ukraine has limited capacity to refurbish stored T-64s on its own, so companies in the Czech Republic and

RIGHT: A Ukrainian T-64BV moves down a muddy trail past a T-80UK captured from the Russians in October 2022. (UKRAINIAN MOD)

WEAPONS OF THE UKRAINE WAR

Poland have signed contracts to do so. Their ability may be limited as both countries produced T-72s, not T-64s. Due to security concerns neither side in the conflict publishes accurate numbers of tanks in service. It is also unknown how many of Ukraine's stored T-64s are too deteriorated to be restored to combat worthiness, though at this point it has many other sources of tanks from NATO nations.

The T-64B still forms the backbone of the Ukrainian tank force, with several sub-models in service. The B model is improved from the older and rarely seen T-64A with a better fire control system, the ability to fire the 9M112 Kobra ATGM from its cannon, and a new gun stabiliser. The T-64BV added explosive reactive armour (ERA) which improved the tank's survivability. The T-64BM Bulat incorporated better ERA, an improved gun capable of firing the Ukrainian Kombat ATGM and a new night sight. Later upgrade on various T-64s includes thermal imagers, satellite navigation units, added armour, better radios, and a more powerful engine.

ABOVE: This Ukrainian T-64BV sports slat armour to defend against RPGs, a 'cope' cage against top attack weapons and a mine clearing device on its front. (UKRAINIAN MOD)

As with other Soviet-era tanks, there are many upgrade packages and it is unknown how many tanks might have a particular improvement, due to component shortages and other issues. Also, as battle-damaged tanks are repaired, they may not receive new upgrades or even get all the equipment they should for the same reason. In wartime, logistics and maintenance suffer.

Compared to the most modern main battle tanks and newer anti-tank weapons, the T-64 is somewhat vulnerable. It is a complex tank, requiring careful maintenance as well. However, it has better cross-country mobility than the T-72 or T-80 and in less likely to get stuck in mud even during the rainy seasons in Spring and Autumn. While it is at a disadvantage against new MBTs, tank versus tank fighting is rare in Ukraine; the T-64 is well suited to infantry support and other missions where its high-explosive rounds can smash enemy fortifications and defences.

T-64BV Characteristics	
Origin	Soviet Union
Crew	3 (commander, driver, gunner)
Length	9.295m (30.5ft)
Height	2.17m (7.1ft)
Engine	700-hp 5TDF diesel
Road Speed	60.5km/h (37.6mph)
Cross Country Speed	35km/h (21.7mph)
Main Gun	125mm 2A26M-1 cannon with 36 rounds
Secondary armament	1 12.7mm NSV machine gun with 300 rounds 1 7.62mm PKT machine gun with 1,250 rounds

BELOW: A trio of Ukrainian T-64s captured by the Russians in April 2022. The Russian Army generally transfers captured T-64s to allied Donetsk and Luhansk troops. (RUSSIAN MOD)

ARMOURED FIGHTING VEHICLES

T-72

Most numerous tank on the battlefield

ABOVE: The PT-91 is a T-72 upgraded by Poland with various bits of European kit added to improve its battle worthiness.
(POLAND MOD)

The T-72 is the most common tank on the battlefields of Ukraine and is used extensively by both armies. This is because it was produced in larger numbers than any other tank in widespread service with the combatants. Even some of the tanks Ukraine is receiving from the West are T-72 variants, acquired from abroad or built in former Warsaw Pact nations.

The T-72 entered service in the Soviet Union in 1973 and soon proliferated through the Warsaw Pact and Soviet client states. It first saw combat during the Iran-Iraq War of 1980-1988 but gained a bad reputation during the 1991 Gulf War. There, it fared poorly against contemporary Western tanks. In fairness, Iraqi T-72s were export models using older, less effective ammunition types and the tanks were poorly maintained.

There are many variants of the T-72, so here we will concentrate on two which are notable for the Ukraine War. There are some shared characteristics, however. The T-72's V-12 diesel engine is considered reliable and, in many ways, more forgiving on maintenance, particularly with inexperienced crews. One observer noted a properly maintained T-72B will start at -20°C even after sitting for a week. Despite criticism, the T-72 is a workhorse tank.

T-72B3: Unable to afford enough T90s for its entire tank fleet, Russia chose to upgrade its T-72Bs, of which it had a large number. The first T-72B3s appeared in 2011 and this type has been gradually improved since, including the T-72B3M. Upgrades include a new gunner's sight, better ERA, the more powerful engine fitted to the T-90, and improved radios and main gun autoloader. The T-72B3/B3M are the most numerous tanks in Russian service; the Army had 983 of them in the months before the February 2022 invasion. Perhaps half that number had been lost by March 2023 and the Russians continue to pull T-72s from storage, upgrade them as far as possible and deploy them to the battlefield. The Ukrainian Army is known to have captured at least 186 and has put some into service.

PT-91 'Twardy': Poland built T-72s under license during the Cold War and during the 1990s devised their own upgraded version, the PT-91 'Twardy' ('Tough'). This variant has a thermal sight, Polish ERA, a more powerful engine, new radios and a laser warning system. Poland transferred 60 PT-91s to Ukraine by mid-2023 and have delivered approximately 250 older T-72s as well.

The T-72s firepower is equivalent to the T-64 or T-80 since they use essentially the same weapons systems. Early model T-72s have a

RIGHT: Dust rises around A Russian T-72B3 as it fires its 125mm cannon. T-72s are known for their relatively low profile, which can make them harder to spot.
(RUSSIAN MOD)

WEAPONS OF THE UKRAINE WAR

WEAPONS OF THE UKRAINE WAR

T-72B3 Characteristics	
Origin	Russia
Crew	3 (commander, driver, gunner)
Length	9.53m (31.3ft)
Height	2.22m (7.3ft)
Engine	840-hp V-84-1
Road Speed	70km/h (43.5mph)
Range	500km (311mi)
Main Gun	125mm 2A46M cannon with 38 rounds
Secondary armament	1 12.7mm NSV machine gun 1 7.62mm PKMT machine gun

ABOVE LEFT: A Russian tank crew 'bombing up,' replenishing their tank's ammunition. Most on-board rounds will be loaded in a carousel which feeds the tank's autoloader. This is probably from a training exercise as the turret machine gun is not fitted. (RUSSIAN MOD)

LEFT: This older-model T-72M1R was donated to Ukraine by Poland. The device in front of the tracks is for mine-clearing. (UKRAINIAN MOD)

BELOW: This T-72B3M has been captured by the Ukrainian Army and put into service. Note the slat armour at the tank's rear and the cloth ERA bags above its tracks. (UKRAINIAN MOD)

slower fire control system, however. One weakness of the T-72 is its poor handling in mud or soft ground. Some T-72s have been abandoned after getting stuck during combat operations.

A notable example was the Battle of Brovary in March 2022. There, a column of the Russian 6th Guards Tank Regiment, with T-72s and other AFVs, was ambushed by Ukrainian forces. When the Russians left the M01 Highway much of the column got stuck in mud. The Ukrainians attacked with ATGM, artillery and UAS, destroying 17 tanks and killing the regimental commander.

There is little information available about the T-72 in Ukrainian service. The army operated a small number alongside their T-64s until the war began in Donbas in 2014. Afterward more T-72s were pulled from storage and refurbished to increase Ukraine tank numbers. This pace accelerated after the 2022 invasion along with about 481 T-72s provided as aid from other nations. At least 200 have been destroyed, damaged or captured during the fighting.

A final note: The T-72 has acquired a reputation for 'popping its top;' i.e., when it suffers a hit which detonates its onboard ammunition, the turret comes flying off, sometimes going several hundred feet into the air. While this has partly to do with the T-72's ammunition stowage scheme and its vulnerability to modern anti-tank weapons, in fairness any tank which suffers major ammunition detonation will likely lose its turret.

www.keymilitary.com

ARMOURED FIGHTING VEHICLES

T-80

The Soviet Union's last tank is still in service

RIGHT: Ukraine makes a variant of the T-80 called the T-84, replacing the gas turbine with a diesel engine. Only a few have been made and most serve with the 14th Mechanised Brigade. (UKRAINIAN MOD)

BELOW: These T-80Us are from the 4th Guards Tank Division, considered an elite formation in the Russian Army. This photo is likely from an exercise, as the heavy machine guns are not mounted on the turret. (RUSSIAN MOD)

The T-80 is the third of the Soviet-era tanks seeing major combat use in Ukraine. It was the most advanced tank the Soviet Union produced before it collapsed. The T-80 was the first tank powered solely by a gas turbine engine, developed when the Soviets learned the US was developing a gas turbine for their next tank, which eventually equipped the M1 Abrams.

This gives the T-80 a reputation as the 'hot rod' of Russian tanks, though it is fuel-hungry. Most of the T-80s in service are T-80Bs or the upgraded T-80Us, which have ERA, better fire control and the capability to fire the Refleks ATGM. Newer T-80Us also have more powerful 1,250hp engines. Gas turbines are much easier to start in cold temperatures; a T-80 can be started and warmed in three minutes compared to 30 minutes for a T-72. Russian units stationed in the far north are issued T-80s for this reason.

Before the invasion of Ukraine in 2022, the Russians counted 443 T-80s in the tank fleet. Ukraine inherited 248 T-80s from the Soviet Union, but kept them in storage until 2014, when they needed more tanks to replace combat losses. The Russians issued T-80s to the 4th Guards Tank Division (4GTD) while the Ukrainians have one ten-tank T80 company in their rapid reaction force units, such as air assault and marine brigades.

4GTD was in the advance on Kharkiv in February 2022. When Ukrainian forces successfully interdicted the Russian supply lines, this unit lacked the fuel for their T-80s and had to abandon many of them, which the Ukrainians captured. The Ukrainians had better luck in September 2022, when their T-80-equipped 25th Airborne and 80th Air Assault Brigades led the Kharkiv counteroffensive. These tanks helped punch through the Russian lines and force a retreat. More T-80s were captured in this action.

T-80U Characteristics	
Origin	Soviet Union/Russia
Crew	3 (commander, driver, gunner)
Length	9.65m (31.7ft)
Height	2.20m (7.2ft)
Engine	1,250-hp GTD-1250
Road Speed	80km/h (49.7mph)
Range	335km (208mi)
Main Gun	125mm 2A46M cannon with 45 rounds
Secondary armament	1 12.7mm machine gun 1 7.62mm PK-series machine gun

40 WEAPONS OF THE UKRAINE WAR

WEAPONS OF THE UKRAINE WAR

T-90

Russia's modern battle tank

T-90MV Characteristics	
Origin	Russia
Crew	3 (commander, driver, gunner)
Length	9.53m (31.3ft)
Height	2.23m (7.3ft)
Engine	1130-hp V-92S2F
Road Speed	60km/h (37mph)
Range	550km (342mi)
Main Gun	125mm 2A46M cannon with 43 rounds
Secondary armament	1 12.7mm NSV machine gun 1 7.62mm PKMT machine gun

Russia created the T-90 during the 1990s to replace the Soviet-era T-64, T-72, and T-80 and be a single main battle tank for the nation. This was an economical solution to having different tanks in inventory, which created logistical and maintenance challenges. After the breakup of the Soviet Union, Russia no longer controlled all the production facilities; having three different tanks which all performed the same tasks made no sense.

At the time, the cash-poor Russians knew their new tank would have to be evolutionary rather than revolutionary; they chose the T-72 as a starting point. The new tank received the designation T-90 to differentiate it from its predecessor. Some argue this was because of the T-72's poor showing against Western tanks during the 1991 Gulf War.

The T-90 incorporates a number of advancements over the T-72 and is altogether a more battle worthy tank. Improvements include a better fire control system, thermal sight and a more powerful engine. It also has ERA and the Shtora ATGM jammer. The T-90 series fixes many of the T-72's flaws.

The most modern version is the T-90M 'Proryv,' or 'Breakthrough.' This latest model incorporates a new 2A46M-5 125mm cannon, an active protection system against ATGM, an 1130-horsepower engine, and a new electronic suite which includes fire control, sighting, visual awareness, and battle management features. The new equipment comes in a new turret. Armour is also upgraded, including more protection around the ammunition carousel for the autoloader. The T-90M was created when production delays plagued the new T-14 Armata, making its debut uncertain.

T-90s have seen extensive service in Ukraine. Many Ukrainian tank troops are complimentary of the T-90M's capabilities and respect what it can do. Its advanced systems make it a formidable opponent. Still, many have been lost or captured. The Russian 27th Guards Motor Rifle Brigade had 20 T-90Ms before the war; captured documents show nine were lost by 15 March 2022 during fighting around Sumy, and more were captured when the Russians were forced back from there. At least one was given to the USA for testing; it was spotted on a flatbed lorry at a petrol station in rural Louisiana during transport!

LEFT: An operational T-90M captured by the Ukrainian 30th Brigade. Note the remote weapon station for the machine gun atop the turret and the tarps and netting used for camouflage. (UKRAINIAN MOD)

BELOW: A Russian T-90S in July 2023. This tank served with the Wagner mercenary group until their June 2023 rebellion and later transferred to the Russian Army. (RUSSIAN MOD)

www.keymilitary.com

ARMOURED FIGHTING VEHICLES

Western Tanks

A mix of old and new

RIGHT: The British Challenger 2 is among the most advanced tanks supplied to Ukraine. Its onboard fire control and battle management systems made it a deadly threat to enemy forces. (UK MOD/CROWN COPYRIGHT)

RIGHT: These Leopard 1A5 tanks are being used to train Ukrainian crews before entering combat. Though lightly armoured, its 105mm gun is effective against the T-72. (UKRAINIAN MOD)

BELOW: A Leopard 2A6 moving at speed during an exercise. Its 120mm main gun is particularly effective against enemy tanks and armoured vehicles. (US ARMY)

The delivery of Western-built tanks to Ukraine has made headlines and been the topic of much discussion regarding how they will fare versus Russian models. In truth tank against tank fighting is rare in conflict and the Ukraine War is no exception. These tanks will be tested in a maelstrom of combat that includes precision weapons, loitering munitions, artillery, mines and a variety of armoured vehicles and anti-tank weapons. There are no wonder weapons; war is a contest of many different weapons wielded in concert through the willpower of the combatants. It is certain the Western nations will observe how their tanks perform on the modern battlefield.

The Western tanks currently promised to Ukraine number around 300, though more may be supplied in the future. Over half of these are Leopard 1A5s, a Cold War design which may better be described as a mobile cannon system than a Main Battle Tank (MBT). Most of the tanks received from the West are T-72s acquired from various sources, refurbished and sent to Ukraine. It is estimated the Ukrainians operate about 1,000 T-64s, T-72s and T-80s.

The Western tanks currently being supplied include the UK's Challenger 2, US M1A1SA, German Leopard 1 and different versions of Germany's popular Leopard 2.

Challenger 2: This British tank entered service in the UK in 1998 and has received periodic updates since then. It saw combat service in Iraq from 2003. Challenger was the first Western MBT promised to Ukraine; notably the UK has taken the lead in supplying advanced weapons to Ukraine, often prompting other nations to do so.

The Challengers serve with the Ukrainian 82nd Air Assault Brigade, which was fighting in the Robotyne-Melitopol area in Southern Ukraine in September 2023. There, it lost one Challenger 2 in action, believed struck by a Kornet missile. The tank first struck a mine and was immobilised, making it an easier

42 WEAPONS OF THE UKRAINE WAR

WEAPONS OF THE UKRAINE WAR

Characteristics of Western Tanks supplied to Ukraine

Model	Leopard 1A5	Leopard 2A6	Challenger 2	M-1A1SA	STRV 122**
Origin	Germany	Germany	United Kingdom	United States	Germany/Sweden
Quantity	165+	21***	14	31	10
Crew*	4	4	4	4	4
Length	9.54m (31.3ft)	9.97m (32.7ft)	8.3m (27.3ft)	9.77m (32ft)	9.97m (32.7ft)
Height	2.7m (8.9ft)	3m (9.8ft)	2.49m (8.2ft)	2.4m (7.9ft)	3m (9.8ft)
Engine	819hp MTU 10 cylinder	1,500hp V-12 turbodiesel	1,200hp V-12 diesel	1,500hp gas turbine	1,479hp V-12 turbodiesel
Road Speed	65km/h (40mph)	70km/h (43.5mph)	59km/h (37mph)	68km/h (42mph)	68km/h (42mph)
Range	600km (373mi)	340km (211mi)	550km (342mi)	550km (342mi)	550km (342mi)
Main Gun	105mm L7A1 with 54 rounds	120mm Rh-120 with 42 rounds	120mm L30A1 with 47 rounds	120mm M256 with 40 rounds	120mm L44 with 42 rounds
Secondary armament	2x7.62 mm Machine guns	2x7.62 mm Machine guns	2x7.62 mm Machine guns	1.50-cal. M2 machine gun 2x7.62mm machine guns	2x7.62 mm Machine guns

* Crew includes commander, gunner, loader and driver
** Strv 122 is a modified Leopard 2A5
*** Ukraine has also received or been promised 54 Leopard 2A4 tanks

target for the Russian missile, which reportedly used a top-attack mode. The crew bailed out, probably before the missile strike. Challengers are prized for long-range firepower and accuracy.

Leopard 1A5: This German 1960s Cold War design entered service in 1986. It uses the famed British L7-series 105mm gun, which is dated against the latest MBTs but still very effective against fixed defences and lighter Armoured Fighting Vehicles (AFVs). The Leopard 1 has notoriously light armour protection and the Ukrainians are reportedly adding ERA to improve survivability. At the time of writing, some Leopard 1A5s are assigned to the new 5th Tank Brigade.

Leopard 2A4/A6 and Strv 122: This is one of the most widely used tanks in Europe. The Germans had over 2100 in service when the Cold War ended and many were subsequently transferred to other countries. Several of these nations have sent Leopard 2s to Ukraine, who added ERA to them to improve survivability. Leopard 2A4s equip a battalion of the 33rd Mechanised Brigade while the 47th Mechanised Brigade uses the Leopard 2A6. These units were seen fighting in Southern Ukraine in late 2023. It appears the Ukrainians have lost around a dozen Leopard 2 with more damaged. The Strv 122 is a Swedish version of the Leopard 2A5. The 21st Mechanised Brigade uses them and was seen fighting in eastern Ukraine in September 2023. Two were damaged by drones in action but one appears to have been repaired and returned to service.

M1A1SA: This is an upgraded version of the original Abrams with better sensors and sights (SA stands for Situational Awareness). This is not the most advanced version of the tank but there are hundreds in storage, allowing more to be transferred if the US chooses. These tanks also lack the uranium armour inserts, which are replaced with tungsten for exported tanks. A social media photo showed a Ukrainian M1 fitted with a remote weapons station for the commander's .50-caliber machine gun. In February-March 2024 Abrams tanks were seen in action with the 47th Mechanised Brigade west of Adiivka in eastern Ukraine. As of early 2024, three have been knocked out, including one lost to a drone striking the tank's roof.

LEFT: Many of the Leopard 2 supplied to Ukraine are the A4 variant shown here. The Ukrainians have fitted some of them with Kontakt-1 reactive armour to improve their protection. (US ARMY)

BELOW: A round flashes from the barrel of an M1A1SA tank. The US provided enough of these tanks to equip a battalion. (US ARMY)

ARMOURED FIGHTING VEHICLES

M-55S

East meets West in this Slovenian T-55 upgrade

RIGHT: A view of M-55S when in service with the 47th Brigade. It appears to have the supporting frames for the reactive armour, but none of the blocks are installed. Also note the curved frames on the tank's rear, for holding fuel drums. (UKRAINIAN MOD)

The M-55S is not a common tank on the battlefields of Ukraine; only 28 were transferred. However, the vehicle is notable as an interesting mix of a Soviet T-55 tank and Western technological upgrades. When Slovenia gained independence from Yugoslavia in 1992, it inherited 30 T-55s. Slovenia chose to upgrade these tanks, as the T-55 was obsolete even in 1992. The Israelis improved many of the Soviet tanks they captured during several wars, so Israeli company Elbit assisted in the program.

These tanks received numerous improvements including an Israeli license-built copy of the famed British L7 105mm cannon. Reactive armour increased the tank's resistance to modern anti-tank weapons and an installed laser warning system would alert the crew and launch the tank's onboard smoke grenades if an aiming laser hit the vehicle. A fire control computer and sights with day and night capabilities dramatically improved the crew's ability to detect and engage targets. The engine was also improved to handle the added weight of the new systems.

The resulting M-55S is a far more capable tank than a T-55, though it is still outclassed by more modern tanks. However, while it would fare poorly in a tank-to-tank engagement, it is perfectly capable of carrying out other roles such as infantry support. It can also take on other older tanks such as the T-62s the Russian are sometimes employing and lightly armoured vehicles such as personnel carriers.

Slovenia transferred these tanks to Ukraine in October 2022 in exchange for some heavy trucks from Germany. After initial issue to the 47th Mechanised Brigade, all 28 M-55S tanks appear to have been transferred to the 67th Mechanised Brigade, fighting in Kremmina in north-eastern Ukraine. There is video evidence from July 2023 of an M-55S struck by a Russian 152mm precision guided artillery shell, which left the tank damaged but drivable. Later that month another M-55S suffered a hit from Russian artillery which set the tank on fire, apparently destroying it. As of March 2024, these tanks were once again transferred to the newly-formed 5th Tank Brigade, also equipped with the Leopard 1A5, which uses the same main gun.

BELOW: An M-55S in Ukrainian service. Additional reactive armour has been added to the tank's sides, along with slat armour to protect the engine compartment. (UKRAINIAN MOD)

M-55S Characteristics	
Origin	Slovenia
Crew	4 (commander, driver, gunner, loader)
Engine	600hp upgraded V-55 diesel
Road Speed	50km/h (31mph)
Range	580km (360mi)
Main Gun	105mm L7-series cannon with 36 rounds
Secondary armament	1 12.7mm DShK machine gun (250 rds.) 1 7.62mm coaxial machine gun (2800 rds.)

44 WEAPONS OF THE UKRAINE WAR

WEAPONS OF THE UKRAINE WAR

Older Soviet-era Tanks

Obsolete but still in the fight

Warfare is a wasteful endeavour. Arsenals of weapons, carefully amassed over decades can be lost in weeks or months. This is happening to both sides in Ukraine; by one account the combined losses total over 3,500 tanks and counting. With such heavy losses and production lines unable to build new tanks to match the loss rates, combatants must improvise.

The Russians are bringing older tanks out of storage, refurbishing them as best they can and sending them into battle. The Soviet Union generally placed even obsolete weapons into long-term storage. Some of those storage facilities are in Ukraine but many more are in Russia, giving it a deep reserve of armoured vehicles.

Thousands of old tanks are available for restoration. They have been sitting without maintenance, generally outside in the Russian weather, in most cases for decades. This means an unknown portion of them are probably deteriorated beyond reasonable repair efforts, but that leaves many able to return to service.

The two older tanks seen in Ukraine are the T-62 and T-55. Neither has the armour protection needed to face a modern tank. They also lack gun stabilisers, meaning they must stop to fire their main gun accurately. They also lack effective night or thermal vision devices.

Still, they have their uses. Many of them are being positioned slightly behind the front lines where they act as artillery support. These tanks do have the ability to conduct indirect fire, and there are reports each tank has but a single soldier manning it, carrying out a slow rate of fire against Ukrainian lines.

One T-55 was packed with six tons of explosives and used as a 'suicide tank,' sent toward enemy lines. It was disabled by a mine, immobilising it before a Ukrainian RPG gunner destroyed it. Reports differ as to whether it was remote-controlled or if Russian troops simply jammed the controls so it would move straight forward.

While these old tanks have little chance against other tanks, they can be useful in the infantry support role, as they can fire useful high-explosive rounds and lay covering fire with their machine guns. Tank against tank battles are quite rare, so these vehicles do have a place, albeit a limited one.

LEFT: This T-62 has been obsolete since the late 1970s but was fitted with a roof cage and sent into battle. It was captured by Ukrainian troops near Kherson in November 2022. (UKRAINIAN MOD)

BELOW: The T-55's 100mm gun is almost useless against modern tanks but could support infantry in attacks on bunkers, trenches or other fixed defences. (US ARMY)

ARMOURED FIGHTING VEHICLES

BMPs

Standard infantry fighting vehicle

ABOVE: BMP-2s of the Russian Army move down a road near Kyiv in March 2022. The lead vehicle has its ATGM mounted on the turret roof.
(RUSSIAN MOD)

This series of armoured vehicles is the most widely produced infantry fighting vehicle (IFV) in the world. In Russian, the acronym BMP translates literally to 'infantry fighting vehicle.' They are used by both sides in the conflict.

IFVs originated during the Cold War to replace the half-tracks, lorries and armoured personnel carriers (APCs) previously used to transport troops on the battlefield. They had heavier armament to support infantry in battle and provided some protection against both enemy fire and Nuclear, Biological and Chemical (NBC) weapons.

The BMP-1 entered service in 1966, surprising Western observers, who were still using APCs. They were soon the standard vehicle for infantry in motor rifle and tank divisions. BMP-1s were also given to Arab states and saw use in the 1973 Yom Kippur War. The Soviets later used them in Afghanistan. Combat experience with the BMP-1 led to upgrades which over time created several distinct models:

BMP-1: The original BMP is praised by users for being fast, agile and having a low profile. It is also cursed for its thin armour, cramped interior and the positioning of the troop seats directly over the fuel tank. The single person turret was too cramped for efficient action in combat. The 73mm gun is also inaccurate past 500 metres. Experience in Afghanistan led to a modernisation program which added belly and side armour and other small improvements. In 2018 the Russian Army adopted the BMP-1AM, which replaces the original turret with that from the BTR-82A fighting vehicle. That turret uses a 30mm autocannon and 7.62mm PKTM machine gun with a day/night sighting system. It is unknown exactly how many BMP-1 were upgraded to this standard, though it appears several dozen have been lost in Ukraine.

BMP-2: The same battle experience which led to the BMP-1's improvements also led to the BMP-2, which introduced a more useful 30mm canon and better ATGM. The turret is enlarged to hold two people, the gunner and commander. It carries thicker armour but carries one less infantryman. Though heavier, the BMP-2's performance is comparable

RIGHT: This BMP-2 of the 74th Guards Motor Rifle Brigade is dug into a hull-down fighting position. Such measures are vital to the survival of this thinly armoured IFV.
(RUSSIAN MOD)

46 WEAPONS OF THE UKRAINE WAR

WEAPONS OF THE UKRAINE WAR

BMP Characteristics				
Model	BMP-1	BMP-2	BMP-3	BMD-2
Origin	Soviet Union	Soviet Union	Soviet Union	Soviet Union
Crew*	3 + 8 troops	3 + 7 troops	3 + 7 troops	2 + 6 troops
Length	6.74m (22.1ft)	6.74m (22.1ft)	7.14m (23.4ft)	5.42m (17.7ft)
Height	2.07m (6.8ft)	2.45m (8ft)	2.4m (7.9ft)	1.97m (6.5ft)
Engine	300 hp V-6 Diesel	300hp V-6 diesel	500hp diesel	241hp six cylinder diesel
Road Speed	65km/h (40.4mph)	65km/h (40.4mph)	70km/h (43.5mph)	80km/h (49.7mph)
Range	600km (373mi)	600km (373mi)	600km (373mi)	600km (373mi)
Primary Armament	73mm cannon with 40 rds	30mm cannon with 500 rds	100mm cannon with 40 rds 30mm cannon with 500 rds	30mm cannon with 300 rds
Secondary Armament	4 Malyutka ATGM 7.62mm PKT machine gun	4 Konkurs ATGM 7.62mm PKT machine gun	6 Bastion ATGM 3x7.62mm PKT machine guns	Konkurs ATGM 7.62mm PKT machine gun

to the BMP-1. The majority of BMPs in both the Russian and Ukrainian armies are BMP-2s, so they are seen frequently on the battlefield.

BMP-3: The third iteration of the BMP is the most heavily armed, with two cannon, ATGM and fully 3 7.62mm machine guns (see table). There are also variants with a different turret sporting a 30mm grenade launcher and a Kornet ATGM launcher. The BMP-3 has better armour protection and can be fitted with ERA. In 2022-2023, The Russians made great efforts to increase production of the BMP-3, hinting at the perceived utility of this version.

BMD-2: This is a lightweight version of the BMP made for airborne forces and able to be parachute dropped. It is armed similarly to the BMP-2 but weighs several tons less due to its thinner armour and smaller size. As with the BMP series, there are other variants of the BMD but there are more BMD-2s in service than any other. Recently some BMD-3s have been spotted on the battlefield. This improved model debuted shortly before the Cold War ended and they were soon placed into storage due to their higher operating costs. The high losses in armoured vehicles in this war likely prompted the vehicle's return from the storage yard.

Over 3,000 BMPs and BMDs have been lost on both sides in this war, primarily due to their thin armour, even on the improved models. Being so numerous, large numbers have been captured on each side as well and are usually returned to service with their new owners. When Russian airborne forces attempted to take Antonov Airport at the beginning of the war, BMDs were spotted among their convoys. For Ukraine, many argue these heavy losses call for increased deliveries of Western IFVs such as the Bradley and CV90, which have better armour protection but are much heavier.

ABOVE: A Ukrainian infantry squad climbs aboard the BMP-2 during training. Soldiers in both armies often ride atop their BMPs due to the danger of a fire or explosion if the vehicle is hit or strikes a mine. (US ARMY)

LEFT: A Ukrainian BMP-1. It is notable few BMP-1s are seen with the Malyutka anti-tank missile fitted over the barrel, likely due to the missile's obsolescence and dwindling stocks. (US ARMY)

LEFT: A knocked-out BMP is an all too common sight in the Ukraine War. This now-derelict BMP-3 sits off a road in Mariupol. (UKRAINIAN MOD)

www.keymilitary.com 47

ARMOURED FIGHTING VEHICLES

BTRs

Wheeled Infantry Fighting Vehicles

ABOVE: The Ukrainian BTR-4 is a heavily armed wheeled IFV. Ukrainian forces used them heavily during the fighting for Bakhmut, prizing their firepower. (UKRAINIAN MOD)

RIGHT: This BTR-80 belongs to the Ukrainian 79th Air Assault Brigade. This appears to be an exercise (note the orange light on the roof, used in training), but it shows how the slat armour is attached to the hull. (US ARMY)

Another design originating from the Soviet Union, the BTR series began as wheeled armoured personnel carriers (APCs). The newest versions have upgraded armament which effectively makes them infantry fighting vehicles (IFVs). The original BTR designs date from the 1950s with the BTR-60, only a few of which have been seen in use in Ukraine. BTR is the Russian acronym for 'armoured transporter.' They are widely used by both sides in the Ukraine War.

The Ukrainians operate hundreds of BTRs while the Russians are believed to have over six thousand, many in storage. As with all weapons in this conflict, many have been lost in action and accurate numbers are effectively impossible to determine. BTRs are reliable and effective in the infantry support role, though as with all such vehicles they are vulnerable to a range of anti-armour weapons. As wheeled vehicles they are less able to handle rough or soft ground compared to tracked vehicles, particularly during the rainy seasons. In dry or frozen conditions this is less of an issue due to their 8-wheel drive and high ground clearance. They are also amphibious.

The standard BTR layout has the driver and commander in the front of the vehicle with the infantry compartment in the middle. The engine is at the rear. There are hatches for troops to exit from the top and doors on each side, allowing troops to exit on one side if the other is under fire. There are four models of BTR primarily in use in Ukraine:

BTR-70: This Cold War mainstay entered service in 1972. It is powered by two petrol engines and is more an APC, carrying a machine gun to support its embarked infantry. Ukrainian industry reportedly refurbished a number of BTR-70s for use by Ukrainian forces. The Russians also possess small numbers of them and they are in use with the Russian-aligned Luhansk and Donetsk military forces.

BTR-80: The weaknesses of the BTR-70 were largely made good in the BTR-80, which replace the twin petrol engines with a single more powerful diesel. It has slightly improved armour protection but is still only proof against small arms fire. Depending on upgrade, its turret carries either a heavy machine gun or 30 mm cannon. The most numerous BTR in the war, there are also variants including command vehicles, mortar carriers and ambulances.

48 WEAPONS OF THE UKRAINE WAR

WEAPONS OF THE UKRAINE WAR

Model	BTR-70	BTR-80	BTR-82A	BTR-4
Origin	Soviet Union	Soviet Union	Soviet Union	Ukraine
Crew	3 + 7 troops	3 + 7 troops	3 + 7 troops	3 + 8 troops
Length	7.54m (24.7ft)	7.7m (25.3ft)	7.7m (25.3ft)	7.76m (25.5ft)
Height	2.32m (7.6ft)	9.5m (8ft)	9.5m (8ft)	3.02m (9.9ft)
Engine	2x120hp gasoline	260hp V8 diesel	300hpV8 diesel	489hp diesel
Road Speed	80km/h (49.7mph)	90km/h (55.9mph)	90km/h (55.9mph)	110km/h (68.3mph)
Range	600km (373mi)	600km (373mi)	600km (373mi)	690km (428mi)
Primary Armament	14.5mm or 12.7mm machine gun	30mm cannon or 14.5mm machine gun	1x30mm 2A72 cannon	1x30mm 2A72 cannon
Secondary Armament	7.62mm PKT machine gun	7.62mm PKT machine gun	7.62mm PKT machine gun	4 ATGM 7.62mm PKT machine gun

LEFT: A Russian BTR moving down a dirt track in Ukraine, April 2022. It has the now-famous 'Z' symbol on the turret and hull sides. (RUSSIAN MOD)

Some improvised versions have also been spotted on the battlefield. One Russian modification placed two 32-round UB-32 rocket pods, normally used by aircraft or attack helicopters, on the vehicle's roof, covered by a 'cope cage' to protect against top attack weapons. Video shows one such BTR struck by armed Ukrainian quadcopter drones. Other BTR-80s are toting remote minelaying systems, turrets salvaged from BMPs and sometimes fire control and sighting systems taken from other armoured vehicles.

BTR-82A: This is essentially an upgraded BTR-80 with better armour, a new 30mm gun turret and more powerful engine. It has a night vision device for the cannon and a satellite navigation system. Some may have thermal imagers as well. The BTR-82AM model is a BTR-80 upgraded to meet BTR-82A standards.

BTR-4: Unlike the other BTR-series vehicles, the BTR-4 is a wholly Ukrainian design with a different configuration. The driver and commander are in the front, engine in the middle and a troop compartment in the rear with an exit ramp for the infantry. It carries a 30mm gun turret at the rear, along with four Konkurs ATGM, two on each side of the turret. Alternately, the ATGM on one side can be replaced with a 30mm grenade launcher. It can be upgraded with added armour or ERA and some have been fitted with slat armour against RPGs.

The Russians also operate a small number of BTR-90s, developed in the 1990s, but not adopted for service. The existing examples were placed in storage and some have since been reactivated and seen in Ukraine.

BELOW: Captured vehicles are often returned to service with the new owner. This formerly Russian BTR-82 received a Ukrainian digital pattern repaint to help distinguish it from enemy vehicles. (UKRAINIAN MOD)

www.keymilitary.com

ARMOURED FIGHTING VEHICLES

Western AFVs

Different vehicles for different missions

ABOVE: The French AMX-10 is a reconnaissance vehicle armed with a 105mm cannon. The Ukrainian marines who use it praise its firepower and good optics but have learned its armour is too thin for direct attacks. (UKRAINIAN MOD)

ABOVE: Ukrainian soldiers pose with their new M2 Bradley IFV in July 2023. Though not invulnerable, the Bradley offers better protection than many similar vehicles and has good firepower and optics. (UKRAINIAN MOD)

ABOVE: The Swedish CV90 carries a squad of infantry and boasts a 40mm autocannon. It is used by the Ukrainian 21st Mechanised Brigade, nicknamed the 'Swedish Brigade' since it uses tanks, IFVs and artillery supplied by that nation. (UKRAINIAN MOD)

ABOVE: The Dutch YPR-765 IFV is an upgraded American M-113 personnel carrier. This one carries a Browning M-2 .50-caliber machine gun; a few have 20mm gun turrets. The Ukrainians received almost 200 of them from the Netherlands. (UKRAINIAN MOD)

RIGHT: The Marder 1A3 is one of the more heavily armoured IFVs transferred to Ukraine. They are issued to the 25th and 82nd Air Assault Brigades. Such units cannot use their helicopters given Russian air defences, so they have converted to mechanised units. (UKRAINIAN AIR ASSAULT FORCES)

50 WEAPONS OF THE UKRAINE WAR

WEAPONS OF THE UKRAINE WAR

ABOVE: The Spartan is a British personnel carrier; many were transferred by the British government but Ukraine states 75 were acquired through private donors. These two examples have been up-gunned with a Mk19 40mm grenade launcher and a Browning M2 .50-calibre machine gun. (UKRAINIAN MOD)

ABOVE: The US is transferring 250 M1117 Armoured Security Vehicles. The armour is light, but the vehicle is heavily armed with a .50-calibre machine gun and 40mm grenade launcher. Its boat-shaped hull will protect the crew against mines as well. (US ARMY)

ABOVE: Almost 1,000 M113 series personnel carriers have been given to Ukraine. It is thinly armoured but easy to maintain. Many of the donated vehicles are medical evacuation variants. (UKRAINIAN MOD)

ARMOURED FIGHTING VEHICLES

MRAPs
Mine Resistant, Ambush Protected

ABOVE: Kirpi is a Turkish designed and built vehicle used by the Ukrainian 35th Marine Brigade. Standard with MRAP-type vehicles, it boat-shaped hull protect the occupants from mines while the armour is proof against small arms fire and grenades. (UKRAINIAN MOD)

ABOVE: Ukrainian Marine units also use British-supplied Mastiff MRAPS. The fast-moving Marines value them for their mine resistance and high speed compared to tracked armoured vehicles. (UKRAINIAN NAVY)

ABOVE: The MaxxPro saw long service in Iraq and Afghanistan and now on the high-intensity battlefields of Ukraine. This one carries a .50-calibre machine gun and appears to have some shrapnel damage to its windscreen. (UKRAINIAN MOD)

RIGHT: The Roshel Senator is a Canadian-made light MRAP, with 1,000 delivered to Ukraine. This example is in use with the Territorial Defence Forces, seen here on exercise. (UKRAINIAN MOD)

52 WEAPONS OF THE UKRAINE WAR

WEAPONS OF THE UKRAINE WAR

Technicals

Improvised vehicles for mobile firepower

ABOVE LEFT: Ukrainian troops have pressed into service numerous civilian vehicles, such as this Peugeot 307 CC. The machine gunner has an L7 GPMG at the ready. (UKRAINIAN MOD)

ABOVE RIGHT: These Nissan pickups are modified to carry American Mk.19 40mm automatic grenade launchers. These vehicles could quickly lay down a barrage of grenades before making a quick escape. (UKRAINIAN MOD)

LEFT: This vehicle was donated by an Estonian organisation and mounts a DShK 12.7mm machine gun. These weapons are frequently used against attacking UAS. (UKRAINIAN MOD)

BELOW: This improvised rocket launcher combines a Nissan pickup with a trailer-mounted B-8M1 rocket pod, usually carried by aircraft. (UKRAINIAN MOD)

www.keymilitary.com 53

ARMOURED FIGHTING VEHICLES

MT-LB Personnel Carrier

A common sight in the Ukraine War

The MT-LB is one of the most numerous and widely used armoured personnel carriers (APCs) in existence, and one of the least noticed. Whenever there is a war somewhere the Soviet Union had influence or simply distributed weapons, the MT-LB went there. If one watches videos of conflicts such as the Ukraine War, eventually a MT-LB full of troops or towing an artillery piece will drive past. They are as ubiquitous as they are disregarded.

There are good reasons to disdain the vehicle. Its armour is only 14mm thick at most, leaving it vulnerable even to some small arms. It was built in the Soviet Union beginning in the early 1970s, making it obsolete. It lacks armament in its basic form, carrying only a medium or heavy machine gun. The engine is loud, so the user gets noticed on the battlefield. As a combat vehicle it is outclassed even by the equally aged BMP-1.

Still, the MT-LB continues in service because there are also many good reasons to use it. It is amphibious and can cross a river at 4mph. Mechanically it is reliable, robust and easy to use. The MT-LB is also versatile, serving as an APC, field ambulance, artillery tractor, mortar carrier, command vehicle, engineer vehicle and weapons carrier.

The vehicle also shows its versatility through the myriad weapons soldiers mount on it, sometimes through purposeful design and other times completely improvised. This happens frequently in Ukraine. MT-LBs have been seen with anti-aircraft guns, ATGM, and gun turrets from IFVs mounted on their hulls. One Ukrainian conversion mounts a 100mm MT-12 anti-tank gun while another uses the BM-7 30mm gun turret from the BTR-4 IFV. The Russians are placing 2M-3 25mm gun turrets from naval vessels on their MT-LBs.

These efforts are partly to make up for combat losses and shortages, but in every war, soldiers improvise weapons useful for themselves in the field. Ukraine is no different. Despite its shortcomings, the MT-LB will continue to be a common sight in the Ukraine War, used by both sides.

RIGHT: One of the most common adaptations for the MT-LB is to mount light antiaircraft guns, such as this ZU-23-2. The weapon is reportedly very effective against ground targets and even drones. (UKRAINIAN MOD)

BELOW: MT-LBs sit on a road near Novoaidar, north of Luhansk in March 2022. The vehicles belong to Russian and Luhansk troops who are meeting before continuing the advance against Ukrainian forces. (RUSSIAN MOD)

MT-LB Characteristics	
Origin	Soviet Union
Crew*	2 + 11 troops
Length	6.45m (21.2ft)
Height	1.86m (6.2ft)
Engine	240hp V-8 Diesel
Road Speed	61km/h (40mph)
Range	500km (310mi)
Armament	7.62mm or 12.7mm machine gun; often seen with improvised weapons

54 WEAPONS OF THE UKRAINE WAR

WEAPONS OF THE UKRAINE WAR

Soviet-era AFVs
Widely used by both armies

ABOVE LEFT: The BTR-MD is a variant of the Soviet-era BMD-3, designed as a multirole armoured personnel carrier. Russian airborne units use them for transport, medical evacuation, command vehicles and carrying supplies. This damaged example was used at the Battle of Hostomel in March 2022. (UKRAINIAN MOD)

ABOVE RIGHT: Ukrainian infantry, supported by a BRDM-2 armoured car armed with a heavy machine gun, during the war in Donbass in 2015. This lightly armoured vehicle is often used for reconnaissance. (UKRAINIAN MOD)

LEFT: The 2S9 Nona-S is based on the BTR-D airborne personnel carrier and mounts a 120mm breech-loading mortar. This weapon can fire ten rounds a minute for short periods. (RUSSIAN MOD)

LEFT: The ZSU-23-4 is designed as an air defence vehicle but sees frequent use against ground targets with its four 23mm cannon. This one is in action with Ukrainian marines in April 2023. (UKRAINIAN MOD)

ARMOURED FIGHTING VEHICLES

TIGR
Infantry Mobility Vehicle

RIGHT: A knocked-out Tigr near Chernihiv in March 2022. This image shows the Tigr's survivability; while the engine and front end are wrecked, the crew compartment appears largely intact, which would help the crew survive.
(UKRAINIAN MOD)

The Tigr serves as Russia's infantry mobility vehicle, a generic term for vehicles with some armour protection and resistance to explosives, but short of what can be found on a wheeled personnel carrier or infantry fighting vehicle. The Tigr is analogous to the UK's Foxhound or the American M-ATV. The Russian designation for the Tir is GAZ-2975.

Tigrs are 4x4s able to handle off-road and limited rough terrain. The Russian military officially adopted it in 2006. It can carry cargo or troops in the rear compartment. The vehicle's features include a central tire inflation system and an engine block heater for cold environments. This is useful as diesel engines require time to warm up before operating, given the Russian and Ukrainian climate.

The most current version is the modernised Tigr-M, with better armour, a more powerful diesel engine, a Nuclear-Biological-Chemical (NBC) filtration system, and a new rear hatch. It can also be fitted with the Arbalet-DM remote weapon station (RWS) atop the vehicle, mounting either a 7.62mm PKTM or 12.7mm Kord machine gun. The system allows the operator to fire the weapon from within the protection of the vehicle, using a laser rangefinder and a small TV camera and thermal imager to locate targets and fire on them.

The Russian military operates thousands of Tigrs and they were seen often during the initial invasion of Ukraine in February 2022. Their speed made them ideal for the sort of lightning-fast victory the Russians hoped to achieve in the first days. Special operations forces and airborne/air assault troops not moving via aircraft or helicopter used them to quickly move toward their objectives. That plan didn't work due to the unexpected and heavy Ukrainian resistance. When faced with heavy anti-armour weapons, Tigrs were outclassed and suffered accordingly.

With the war entering its third year, the Tigr is seen less often on the battlefield due to this vulnerability, though it is still useful for rear-area transport and security duties. For support roles several Tigr variants exist. These include an anti-aircraft vehicle carrying four small missiles on a retractable mount, a radar carrier and an electronic warfare vehicle.

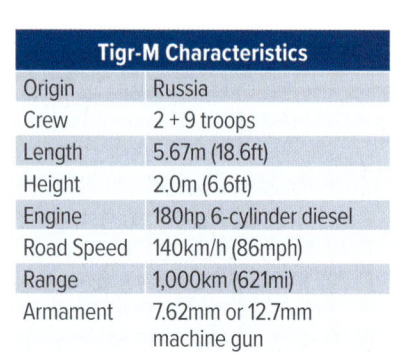

BELOW: While these Tigr-Ms do not appear to be anywhere near a combat zone, this image shows the remote weapon station with its 12.7mm machine gun and smoke grenade dischargers in detail.
(RUSSIAN MOD)

Tigr-M Characteristics	
Origin	Russia
Crew	2 + 9 troops
Length	5.67m (18.6ft)
Height	2.0m (6.6ft)
Engine	180hp 6-cylinder diesel
Road Speed	140km/h (86mph)
Range	1,000km (621mi)
Armament	7.62mm or 12.7mm machine gun

WEAPONS OF THE UKRAINE WAR

Engineer Vehicles

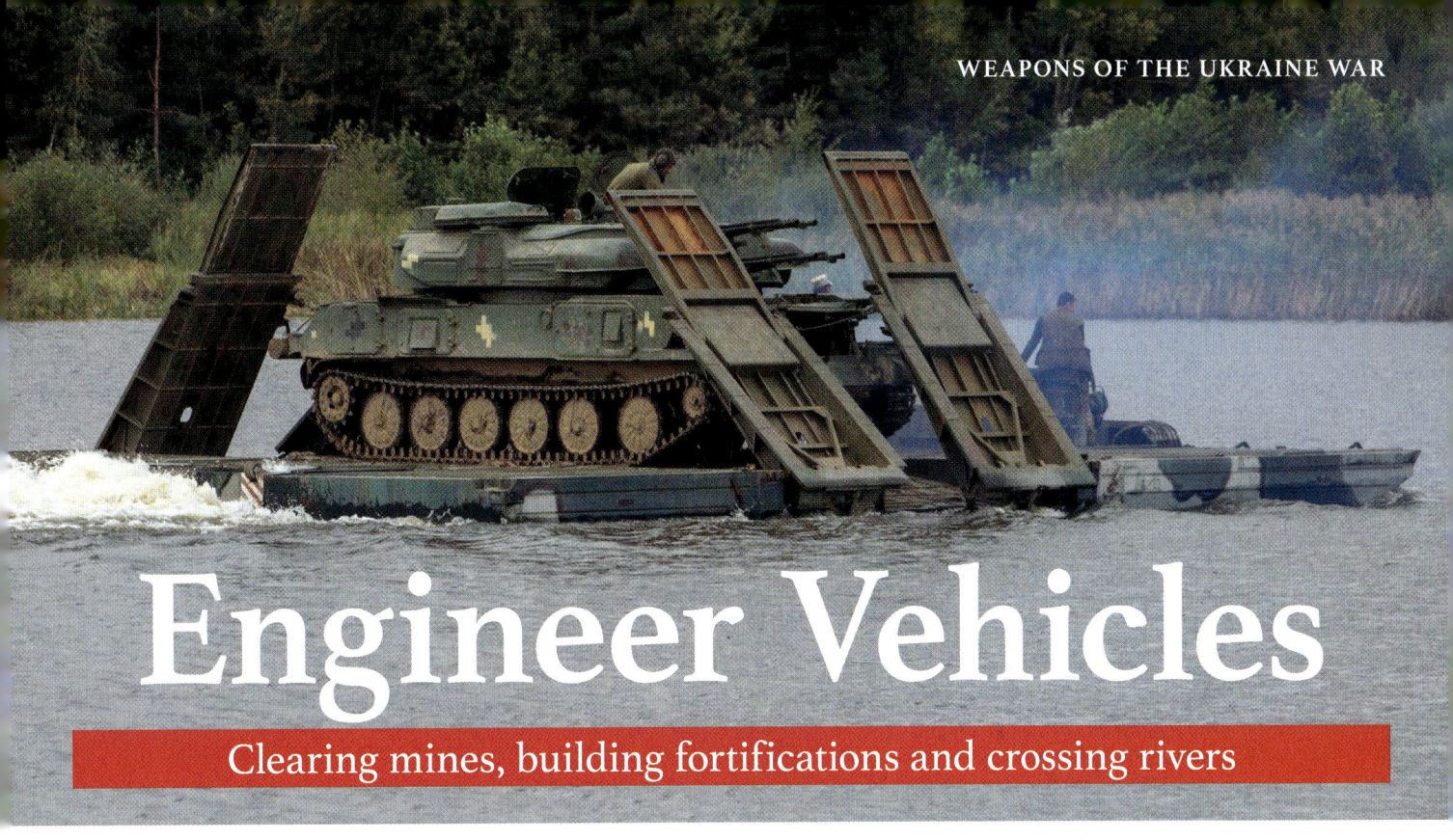

Clearing mines, building fortifications and crossing rivers

ABOVE: Many rivers are too wide for armoured bridgelayers. Here a raft transports a Ukrainian ZSU-23-4 air defence vehicle. (US ARMY)

LEFT: The UR-77 mine clearing vehicle uses a rocket-propelled line charge to clear lanes through minefields. When the charge detonates it disable mines in a path 90 meters long by 6 meters wide. (RUSSIAN MOD)

BELOW LEFT: The BAT-2 combat engineer vehicle, used by both sides, carries an adjustable dozer blade at the front, a soil ripper spike at the rear and a 2-ton crane on top. It is based on the T-64 tank chassis. (US ARMY)

BELOW RIGHT: For narrow waterways or large ditches bridgelayers such as this Russian TMM-3M are valuable assets. It carries four 10.5-meter bridge sections. (RUSSIAN MOD)

ARTILLERY

HIMARS and MLRS

Precision rocket firepower

RIGHT: A Ukrainian soldier sitting at the fire control panel of a French-supplied MLRS launcher. Note the metal slats over the windscreen for added protection. (UKRAINIAN MOD)

These advanced Western rocket launchers are another of the highly publicised weapons supplied to Ukraine in this war. They bring a long legacy of combat effectiveness, first used on the battlefield during the Gulf War in 1991. Iraqi soldiers who had to endure MLRS bombardments soon gave it the grim sobriquet 'Steel Rain.'

Ironically, the United States developed the tracked M270 MLRS system to destroy massed Soviet armoured formations during the anticipated invasion of Western Europe during the Cold War. MLRS proved so effective the US later created the wheeled M142 HIMARS as a lightweight, more portable weapon.

Now both systems are in use against Russia, though massed formations are uncommon. The UK, Germany, Italy, Norway and France provided an estimated 23 of the tracked M270-series launchers. It is heavier, slightly better armoured, carries two pods of six rockets each or two ATACMS missile pods with one missile each and has better survivability on the battlefield.

The wheeled M142 HIMARS, provided by the United States (both vehicles are US designed), lacks the cross-country mobility of its tracked counterpart but is much lighter and can be air-transported even on a C-130-sized aircraft. Wheeled vehicles are less complex than tracked vehicles, so HIMARS are generally more reliable and less maintenance intensive. Being smaller it carries a single rocket or missile pod.

Both types are very mobile, an advantage in Ukraine where

BELOW: A HIMARS firing in Ukraine. The flash and smoke from a launch can be seen at long distances and the launch detected by radars, meaning the crew must move immediately. (UKRAINIAN JOINT FORCES COMMAND)

Rocket and Missile ammunition in use by Ukraine		
Type	Warhead	Range (km)
GLSDB with M26 Rocket	93 kg (205 lb)	150
M31 Guided	200 lb unitary	92
M39 ATACMS	950 bomblets	165

58 WEAPONS OF THE UKRAINE WAR

WEAPONS OF THE UKRAINE WAR

UAS, artillery radars and modern battlefield reconnaissance systems can quickly bring attacks and counterbattery fire. They can fire a salvo and immediately move away, usually to a camouflaged reload point so the vehicle can exchange their now-empty pods for fresh ones and be ready for the next fire mission. A rocket or missile pod can be reloaded in 10-15 minutes.

Older MLRS rockets, particularly the M26, are cluster munitions carrying hundreds of submunitions. These submunitions have a low but definite dud rate, meaning a few submunitions from each rocket become unexploded munitions littering the battlefield, posing a danger to civilians and troops alike. The US and many other nations have eliminated or restricted use of these rockets.

Conversely, cluster munitions are very effective and with the exigencies of the war, there are discussions about transferring M26 rockets to Ukraine. The thought is that dud munitions, which are unfortunately already numerous anyway, can be cleaned up later, but only if the war is won. Another rocket type, the M30A2, replaces submunitions with 182,000 tungsten fragments, and has been very effective in Ukrainian hands.

Most of the rockets and missiles provided to Ukraine carry unitary warheads, a single explosive device per missile which, using precision targeting, are effective against command posts, logistics and ammunition depots, airfields and aircraft shelters. The M-31 Guided MLRS rocket, also called the GMLRS or 'Gimler,' uses GPS guidance and is the most common rocket supplied to Ukraine so far.

In 2023 the US approved transfer of the Army Tactical Missile System (ATACMS), which can be used by both MLRS and HIMARS launchers. It appears the version sent is the M39, an older variant with a shorter range and a cluster munition warhead. It is also supplying the US-Swedish Ground-Launched Small Diameter Bomb (GLSDB), which can be launched via a modified M26 rocket (no cluster munitions) from either launcher. This bomb can penetrate up to three feet of reinforced concrete and has precision capability. They are scheduled for delivery in early 2024.

In action HIMARS/MLRS has proven effective, able to fire and quickly move before counterbattery fire responds, generally three to five minutes. They have particular use against Russian command posts and vehicles, ammunition depots and opposing artillery and air defence units. However, the Russians can use electronic warfare assets to jam the GPS signals the GMLRS uses, degrading its accuracy. As of this writing, only one MLRS or HIMARS launchers is known to have been destroyed, though a photograph of a HIMARS with possible mine damage has been seen. The Ukrainians appear to be cautious and deliberate in how they employ them to reduce the risk of loss.

MLRS/HIMARS Characteristics		
Type	M270 MLRS	M142 HIMARS
Origin	United States	United States
Mass	25,000kg (55,100lb)	16, 239 kg (35,800 lb)
Length	6.85m (22.5ft)	7m (23ft)
Crew	3	3
Rate of fire	1 round every 6 seconds	1 round every 6 seconds
Rocket tubes	12 227mm rockets or two missiles	6 227mm rockets or one missile

ABOVE: A French-supplied MLRS with its Launcher-Loader Module in firing position. After firing the module is quickly rotated into travel position and the crews drives to a reload point. (UKRAINIAN MOD)

LEFT: In this still from a Ukrainian video, HIMARS launchers carry out a fire mission near Zaporizhia in June 2022. The launcher can stop on the road for a sudden fire mission before quickly moving away. (UKRAINIAN MOD)

ARTILLERY

BM-27 Uragon and BM-30 Smerch

Long range rocket artillery

ABOVE: The BM-30 is one of the longest-ranged MLRS systems in the world. Like all such systems, it produces extensive flash and smoke when firing. (US DOD)

RIGHT: In the still image taken from video, Ukrainian artillery soldiers train with their BM-27s shortly before the war began in February 2022. (UKRAINIAN JOINT FORCES COMMAND)

These two systems provide long range rocket artillery support for both the Russian and Ukrainian forces. The Soviet Union created both weapons to supplement the large number of relatively short-ranged BM-21 122mm system used by the Red Army and Warsaw Pact forces. Larger calibre rocket launchers not only increased firing range but allowed larger and different types of warheads.

The BM-27 Uragon fires a 220mm rocket from a 16-tube launch assembly originally mounted atop an 8x8 ZIL truck chassis. There are several warhead types including high explosive fragmentation, anti-tank, bomblet and even anti-tank mines. Range is 35km. An updated version called the Uragan-1M serves in the Russian army. It uses a new truck chassis and reportedly fires extended range rockets out to 70km. Ukraine also produces an updated BM-27 called the Bureviy. This version uses a Tatra truck chassis, is equipped with a digital fire control system and rockets with a range of 65km.

The BM-30 Smerch is even larger, firing 300mm rockets from a 12-tube launcher out to 70 km. The standard rocket has a high explosive fragmentation warhead but a rocket with submunitions exists. Russia used the Smerch to develop the 9K515 Tornado-S. Like the Tornado upgrade to the BM-21, this new system uses an automatic fire control system and a GLONASS satellite navigation receiver for improved accuracy. It uses both the same rockets as the Smerch and new versions, some of them guided, with 120km range. Ukraine has a Smerch update called the Vilkha with a range of 130km.

The long range of these two systems make them ideal for attacking targets behind the frontline, such as command posts and supply depots. Like most MLRS they increase survivability by moving immediately after firing. Ukraine used its Bureviy launcher against the Russians near Kharkiv in August 2022.

BM-27 and BM-30 Characteristics		
Type	BM-27	BM-30
Origin	Soviet Union	Soviet Union
Mass:	20,000kg (44,092lb)	17,982kg (39,644lb)
Length:	8.75m (24.1ft)	12m (39.4ft)
Crew	6	3
Rocket tubes	16 220mm tubes	12 300mm tubes
Maximum firing range	70km (43.5mi)	120km (74.5mi)

WEAPONS OF THE UKRAINE WAR

WEAPONS OF THE UKRAINE WAR

RM70

An update of a classic Soviet weapon

RM-70 Characteristics	
Origin	Czech Republic
Mass:	33,697kg (74,290lb)
Length:	8.75m (24.1ft)
Crew	6
Rate of fire:	1 round every 0.5 seconds
Rocket tubes	40 122mm tubes
Maximum firing range	Range varies by rocket type: Standard rocket: 20km 9M521: 40km

During the Cold War the Warsaw Pact was liberally supplied with the BM-21 rocket launcher (see pages 62-63) by the Soviet Union. Often these countries produced Soviet designs in their own factories. Sometimes the new manufacturer would add their own improvements or derive an improved model.

The RM-70 is an example of a locally made upgrade. Made in then-Czechoslovakia, the RM-70 derives from the BM-21. It fires the same 122mm rockets, able to use any of the Soviet or Russian types along with two locally made designs. The standard rocket uses a high explosive fragmentation warhead, but there are variants with anti-armour submunitions, anti-tank mines or anti-personnel mines.

The basic launcher uses a 6x6 truck chassis with a 40-tube launch assembly at the rear. The major difference for the RM-70 is a 40-rocket reload package between the launch tubes and the truck's cab. This allows the crew to quickly reload for a second salvo without needing an ammunition truck or needing to move to a specific reloading point.

The Czech Republic supplied 20 RM-70s in July 2022. They also transferred an estimated 20 more of an improved version called the RM-70 Vampire. It uses a new truck chassis with a more powerful drivetrain and a new digital fire control system. The crew cabin has better armour protection.

Since the RM-70 is like the BM-21 in most respects it fits well into the Ukrainian artillery forces, who use the BM-21 extensively. Ukrainian troops have reported favourably on the RM-70, considering it superior to the BM-21. In a video shared online, a Ukrainian soldier stated using the RM-70 is akin to replacing 'a Soviet car with a Western one." In January 2024 the Russian MoD stated the RM70 Vampire was used in an attack on Belgorod, saying Russian air defences intercepted between seven and 10 of the rockets along with Ukrainian UAS. At the time of writing, Ukraine had not confirmed the attack.

BELOW: A Ukrainian crew lays in their RM-70. Gun laying procedures accurately provide the launcher's location, improving accuracy. (UKRAINIAN MOD)

BELOW: Artillerymen of the 110th Mechanised Brigade firing their RM-70 rocket launchers. The vehicle can set up, fire and move within three minutes. (UKRAINIAN MOD)

ARTILLERY

BM-21 Grad

Legacy rocket artillery system.

RIGHT: A Russian BM-21 battery conducting firing exercises. Massing the fire of multiple launchers inflicts terrible destruction on a target area. (RUSSIAN MOD)

The Grad ('Hail' or 'Hailstorm') is a lorry-mounted 122mm rocket system which entered service in the Soviet Union in 1963. Despite it age and relative unsophistication, it remains the most common rocket artillery weapon in use with both the Russian and Ukrainian armies. They have seen combat use since 2014 in the Donbas.

The Grad remains in service because it is a simple, durable artillery weapon effective for area target missions. A single launcher can fire 40 122mm rockets in about 20 seconds out to 20km distance with standard rockets. At that range the rockets will disperse, blanketing an area up to 600 by 600 meters with high explosive fragmentation warheads. It is not a precision weapon, as firing causes the launcher's suspension to move, affecting each rocket's flight and accuracy.

The weapon is also very mobile; after firing the crew simply drives the launcher away to avoid counter battery fire, often gone before the rockets impact. A resupply lorry with 60 rockets accompanies each launcher. Both are 6x6 lorries for good cross-country performance. It takes about ten minutes to reload the launcher. Both armies organise their BM-21s into batteries of four to six launchers, enabling them to concentrate devastating barrages against a target very quickly.

The standard rocket for the BM-21 is the 9M22, a high explosive fragmentation rocket designed to create 3,920 fragments. There are several other explosive rockets in service, including one in which the warhead separates from the rocket and descends on a parachute, exploding at a pre-set height. There are also long-range rockets with a range of 40km, smoke and radio jamming rockets.

Russia also operates an improved launcher called the Tornado-G. Visually it looks very similar to the BM-21 but incorporates several major upgrades. It has satellite navigation for precise positioning, and more sophisticated fire control systems. Tornado-Gs can fire the BM-21's rockets or its own versions with longer range and more powerful warheads. After firing it moves from the launch point like the BM-21 but can reload its launch tubes in seven minutes.

Russia is believed to have over two thousand BM-21s, with most

BELOW: A Ukrainian launch crew sights in their BM-21. While the weapon lacks accuracy, good artillery weapon laying techniques will reduce the dispersion. (UKRAINIAN JOINT FORCES COMMAND)

WEAPONS OF THE UKRAINE WAR

BM-21 Grad Characteristics	
Origin	Soviet Union
Mass	13,700kg (30,203lb)
Length	7.35m (24.1ft)
Crew	3
Rate of fire	1 round every 0.5 seconds
Rocket tubes	40 122mm tubes
Maximum firing range	Range varies by rocket type Standard 9M22 rocket: 20km 9M521: 40km

LEFT: A Russian crew aiming their Tornado-G. This version looks much like a BM-21 but has fire control upgrades to make it more accurate.
(RUSSIAN MOD)

of them in storage. It is unknown how many are currently in service, given combat losses and reactivation of stored systems. Ukraine had 184 BM-21s before the 2022 phase of the war began. The Russians also possessed about 180 Tornado-G launchers in 2022.

The BM-21 sees frequent use on Ukrainian battlefields. One of the most famous uses occurred in July 2014 near Zelenopillia in Luhansk. A Ukrainian column assembled in a field near the village roughly nine km from the Russian border. The column included elements of the 24th and 72nd Mechanised Brigades and the 79th Airmobile Brigade. The Russians fired salvos of Tornado-G rockets from a position on the Russian side of the border, as determined by a later investigation. The Ukrainian column suffered terrible losses, 37 dead and 100 wounded. A unit member claimed the airmobile element was almost entirely destroyed.

Some Ukrainian troops say the BM-21 is old and unreliable, as the launchers break down often, likely due to age. At least one Ukrainian artillery unit nicknamed their BM-21s 'Grandma.' However, they do provide heavy firepower and are ideal against massed enemy attacks. Ukraine does not operate the Tornado-G, excepting any operable examples they may have captured. There are also examples of improvised rocket launchers built by taking the 122mm rocket tubes from a disabled Grad and mounting them on pickups, lorries and trailers.

Both sides consider the BM-21 and other rocket systems as high-value targets and hunt them with UAS and other target acquisition systems. Any that are located will be attacked quickly.

BELOW: A Ukrainian BM-21 firing a salvo. Rockets are easily detected by enemy counterbattery radars, so this crew will move immediately after the last rocket is fired.
(UKRAINIAN MOD)

www.keymilitary.com

ARTILLERY

2S19 Msta

Russia's modern self-propelled gun

RIGHT: Russian 2S19s firing on a target. This is likely a training exercise as the vehicles are out in the open and have ammunition boxes scattered behind them.
(RUSSIAN MOD)

The 2S19 Msta, named for a Russian river, entered Soviet service in 1989, near the end of the Cold War. There is also a towed gun named the 2A65 Msta; the Russian designation system denotes a Self-Propelled Gun (SPG) with the letter S and towed guns with the letter A. It uses automotive and chassis components from the T-72 and T-80 tanks combined with a large turret holding a 152mm howitzer. The turret has a 360-degree traverse and is mounted in the centre of the hull, unlike most SPGs which have rear-mounted turrets.

Russia also has a modernised version called the 2S33 with an improved cannon capable of longer range, a better fire control system and a rate of fire of 10 rounds per minute. Most reports on 2S19s in action do not differentiate between it and the 2S33, which is also known as the 2S19M2.

Along with its predecessor, the 2S3 Akatsiya, the 2S19 is the most numerous SPG in Russian service; Russia had about 800 of each in service before the war began in 2022. Somewhere around 200 of their 2S19s have been destroyed or captured. Ukraine had around three dozen 2S19s before the invasion and captured perhaps 50 more, mostly during the Ukrainian counteroffensive in the second half or 2022. It is unknown how many of them were still operable.

The 2S19 is an effective and long-ranged cannon system, which makes it a priority target for either army. Its survivability is mainly due to its mobility, as its armour is only 15mm, though no SPG has armour thick enough to withstand direct hits from anti-tank weapons. Numerous videos can be found online showing 2S19s in action and being attacked by UAS, HIMARS, artillery and precision munitions.

BELOW: A battery of Ukrainian 2S19s on the move during the Donbas War in 2015. Since the separatists and Russians also used the 2S19, the recognition flags are important to avoid 'friendly' fire.
(UKRAINIAN MOD)

2S19 Self-Propelled Gun Characteristics	
Origin	Soviet Union
Mass:	42,184kg (93,000lb)
Length:	7.15m (23.5ft)
Crew	5 personnel
Rate of fire:	6-8 rounds per minute
Maximum firing range	24.7km (15.3mi) standard round 36km (22.3mi) using rocket assisted projectile (RAP)

WEAPONS OF THE UKRAINE WAR

2S1 Gvozdika

Light howitzer

Russian for 'Carnation,' the Gvozdika is unusual on the modern battlefield due to its relatively small calibre 122mm howitzer. This was the standard Soviet light howitzer during the Cold War, while the Soviet's NATO opponents standardised on the 105mm howitzer. Most currently produced SPGs mount larger cannon, 152mm for Russian pattern weapons and 155 mm for guns modelled after US and NATO designs. The Ukrainian name is 'Hvozdyka.'

The 2S1 is based on the chassis of the successful MT-LB personnel carrier. The driver sits on the vehicle's front left with the 300hp V-8 diesel on the right. The turret is mounted at the rear, the most common arrangement for SPGs, allowing the rear hatch to be used for crew access, ammunition loading ('bombing up') and maintenance. The vehicle is amphibious, requiring a few minutes to erect screens around the engine intakes and activate a small bilge pump. Like most SPGs, the armour only protects against small arms fires and artillery shrapnel.

The vehicle first entered service in 1971 and stayed in production until the Soviet Union dissolved in 1991; over 10,000 were produced and it was a standard SPG in tank and motor rifle divisions. They were manufactured in Kharkiv and widely distributed to Soviet client states.

Hundreds of 2S1s are in service in both the Russian and Ukrainian armies and the Russians are believed to have over 1,000 in storage. Artillery ammunition shortages are common in this war; one Ukrainian advantage is their ability to manufacture 122mm ammunition, making them less dependent on foreign aid for this type. For the Russians, the 2S1 is popular with the Naval Infantry due to its light weight and amphibious capability.

ABOVE: A 2S1 SPG of the Ukrainian 128th Transcarpathian Brigade in November 2022. (UKRAINIAN MOD)

LEFT: The pixelised camouflage pattern on this 2S1 shows it is in Ukrainian service. This vehicle is with the 59th Motorised Brigade, firing its gun in September 2022. (UKRAINIAN MOD)

LEFT: Russian Naval Infantry using the 2S1 during a landing exercise in 2015. With proper preparation, the 2S1 can swim out to the landing ship in the distance. (RUSSIAN MOD)

2S1 Self-Propelled Gun Characteristics	
Origin	Soviet Union
Mass:	16,000kg (35,273lb)
Length:	7.26m (23.8ft)
Crew	4 personnel
Rate of fire:	1-2 rounds per minute sustained 5 rounds per minute maximum
Maximum firing range	15.2km (9.4miles) standard round

www.keymilitary.com 65

ARTILLERY

2S7 Pion/2S7M Malka

Heavy-hitting artillery

RIGHT: The powerful 203mm cannon on the 2S7 creates substantial muzzle flash. Note the spade dug-in behind the vehicle to absorb recoil. The white tubes on the right are storage containers for ammunition.
(UKRAINIAN MOD)

The 2S7 Pion 203mm SPG entered service in the Soviet Union in the mid-1970s. Pion is the Russian word for the Peony flower. The 2S7 is the largest cannon artillery system in use in the Ukraine War (Russia does operate a 240mm mortar system). Both Ukraine and Russia operate it.

The 2S7 is a large vehicle, with a chassis based on the T-72 and T-80 tanks. Its long-barrelled 203mm cannon is capable of long-range firing, particularly with rocket assisted projectiles. Projectiles include high explosive, concrete piercing and even tactical nuclear rounds (for the Russians). The vehicle mounts a front dozer blade to help the crew dig a protected firing position while a recoil spade at the rear helps the crew deal with the tremendous recoil produced by firing.

The weapon has a large crew of 14 soldiers, providing plenty of muscle for loading its ammunition, which weighs 110kg. A second vehicle accompanies the first to carry half the crew and extra ammunition, as the 2S7 only carries four rounds. Russia developed a modernised version called the 2S7M Malka. This version has a new engine, transmission and an improved fire control system.

BELOW: In this image taken from video, 2S7s of the Ukrainian 43rd Artillery Brigade rush through Kyiv on the morning of 22 February 2022 to engage Russian paratroopers at Antonov Airport. (UKRAINIAN MOD)

2S7 Self-Propelled Gun Characteristics	
Origin	Soviet Union
Mass:	46,600kg (102,735lb)
Length:	10.5m (34.4ft) when deployed for firing
Crew	14 personnel
Rate of fire:	1-2 rounds per minute (sustained)
Maximum barrel elevation	60 degrees
Maximum firing range	37.5km (23.3 miles) standard; 47.5km (29.5 miles) using rocket assisted projectile (RAP)

The primary advantage of the 2S7 is its long range, reportedly up to 47,500 m with rocket assisted projectiles. Ammunition supply is a concern for Ukraine as it lacked an extensive stockpile before the war. However, the US pledged to supply 10,000 203mm rounds; at least some of these are US-made projectiles for its M110 howitzer, taken out of service in the mid-1990s. It is also possible the US located and purchased ex-Soviet ammunition.

2S7s have been in combat since the beginning of the war. In 2014 Ukraine reactivated some to fight in the Donbass. When Russian paratroopers seized Antonov Airport in February 2022, 2S7s from the 43rd Artillery Brigade fired on the runway, cratering it and preventing the Russians from flying in reinforcements. Satellite imagery has revealed Russian 2S7s near the front line in Donetsk. Russian news releases state it uses the 2S7 in concert with the Orlan-10 UAS for target location and attack.

66 WEAPONS OF THE UKRAINE WAR

WEAPONS OF THE UKRAINE WAR

2A36 Giatsint-B

Towed field gun

The Giatsint ('Hyacinth') is a large, towed field gun. In artillery terms, field guns generally have longer barrels and fire at a lower angle, while howitzers are usually shorter-barrelled and fire at high elevation angles. It entered service in the Soviet Union in 1975 as a long-range gun for counter-battery fire and deep artillery strikes.

The gun has a crew of eight troops, mainly to provide manpower to move the weapon's large ammunition type. These rounds utilise a separate projectile with a casing containing the propellant charges. The projectile is loaded into the weapon first and the casing rammed into place afterward. This ammunition is not compatible with other 152mm ammunition in use in other artillery systems. For example, the casing in the Giatsint is much larger than that used in the 2S19 self-propelled gun, which is also in 152mm calibre.

There is a variety of ammunition available including high explosive, illumination, smoke, and even armour-piercing. As a towed cannon, the 2A36 takes longer to set up for firing and to displace after firing. This makes it more vulnerable to counter battery fire and UAS attack, as it may not be able to move before enemy fire arrives. Relatively rare on modern artillery, the Giatsint also has a large shield to protect the crew against incoming fire from the front.

Both the Russian and Ukrainian armies operate the 2A36 in considerable numbers and the Russians are believed to have more in storage. Ukraine used them in the Donbass in 2014-15 and continued their use up to the present conflict. Finland donated an unknown number of their version of the Giatsint, known as the K89, to Ukraine in early 2023.

2A36 152mm Field Gun Characteristics	
Origin	Soviet Union
Mass:	9,761kg (21,520lb)
Length:	12.3m (40.3ft) when deployed for firing
Crew	8 personnel
Rate of fire:	6 rounds per minute (maximum)
Maximum firing range	30.5km (18.9 miles) standard; 40km (24.8 miles) using rocket assisted projectile (RAP);

ABOVE: Ukrainian artillerymen fire two Giatsints during the Donbass War in 2016. Artillery duels were common in that phase of the war. (UKRAINIAN MOD)

BELOW: This Ukrainian crew loads their Giatsint. Note the very large shell casing, which holds the propellant charge. The casing is ejected after firing and a soldier holding the wooden pole will push the hot casing out of the crew's way. (UKRAINIAN MOD)

THE DESTINATION FOR AVIATION ENTHUSIASTS

Visit us today and discover all our publications

Aviation News is renowned for providing the best coverage of every branch of aviation.

Air International has established an unrivalled reputation for authoritative reporting across the full spectrum of aviation subjects.

SIMPLY SCAN THE QR CODE OF YOUR FAVOURITE TITLE ABOVE TO FIND OUT MORE!

FREE P&P* when you order

shop.keypublishing.com

Call +44 (0)1780 480404 *(Mon to Fri 9am - 5.30pm GMT)*

451/24

SUBSCRIBE TODAY!

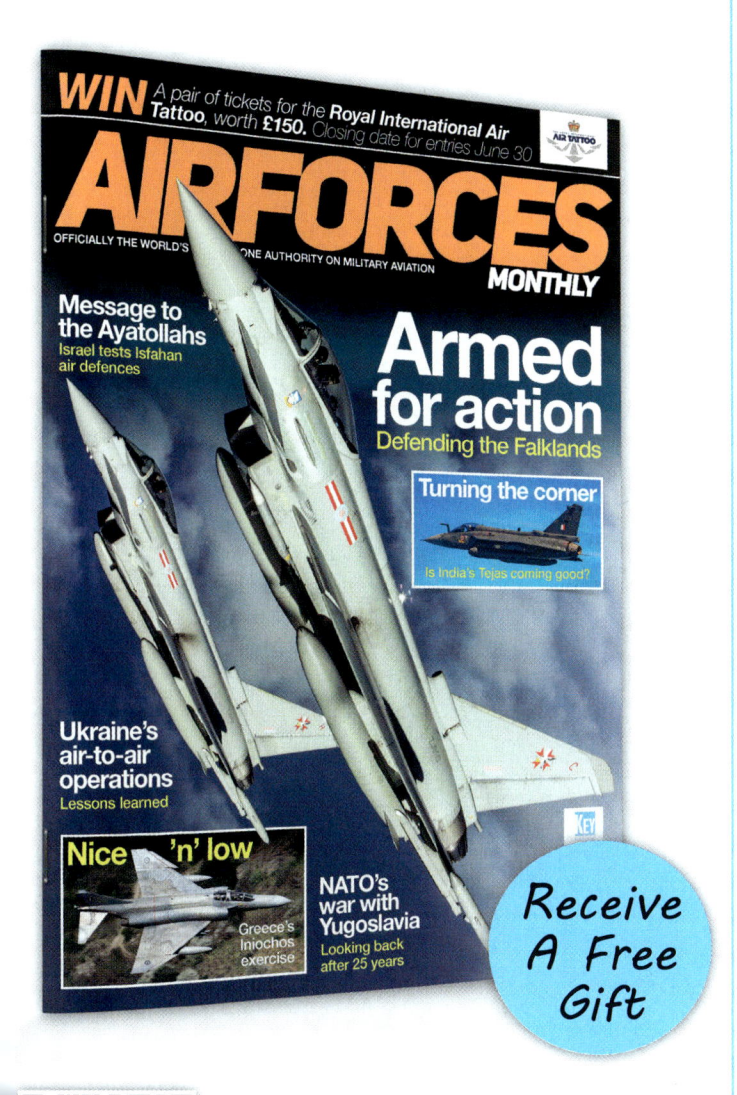

Receive A Free Gift

Receive A Free Gift

Airforces Monthly is devoted to modern military aircraft and their air arms.

Combat Aircraft Journal is renowned for being America's best-selling military aviation magazine.

from our online shop...
/collections/subscriptions

*Free 2nd class P&P on all UK & BFPO orders. Overseas charges apply.

ARTILLERY

AHS Krab

Poland's 155 mm howitzer

RIGHT: The Krab's long barrelled 155mm cannon provides longer range over older 155mm gun systems. The support helps relieve stress on the barrel during movement. (UKRAINIAN MOD)

The AHS Krab is a Polish self-propelled gun (SPG), one of several designs transferred to Ukraine by Western nations soon after the war began in 2022. AHS is a Polish abbreviation for 'howitzer, self-propelled.' Poland gave 18 Krabs to Ukraine in May 2022. Soon after Ukraine signed an agreement to purchase another 60 Krabs and that appears to be a mix of transfers from the Polish Army and new production.

The Krab is unusual in that it combines the turret from the UK's AS90 with the chassis of the South Korean K9 Thunder SPG, produced under license in Poland. The fire control system is Polish. The cannon is a Rheinmetall-designed 155mm 52-calibre gun. When describing cannon, calibre in this sense means the length of the barrel is 52 times the diameter of the ammunition size; in this example, 52 x 155 equals 8060 mm, or 8.06 meters (26.4 feet).

In June 2022 Ukraine reported using Krab SPGs during the Battle of Sievierodonetsk. Interior Minister Roscislav Smirnov credited the Krab with helping to stabilise the lines around the embattled city, though it fell to Russian forces soon after. The Krab's long barrelled cannon allowed it to engage targets beyond the range of other Ukrainian artillery, particularly their Soviet-era guns. There are also reports the Ukrainians can fire the US-made Excalibur precision artillery shell from the Krab.

BELOW: The forest provides some concealment from hostile UAS and other enemy reconnaissance forces. The Krab can quickly move out to a firing position, then fall back into hiding to avoid counterstrikes. (UKRAINIAN GROUND FORCES)

AHS Krab Self-Propelled Gun Characteristics	
Origin	Poland
Mass:	48,080kg (105,998lb)
Length:	12.1m (39.7ft) when deployed for firing
Crew	5 personnel
Rate of fire:	2 rounds per minute (sustained) 6 rounds per minute (maximum)
Maximum barrel elevation	70 degrees
Maximum firing range	30km (18.6 miles) using rocket assisted projectile (RAP); 40km (24.8 miles) using Excalibur precision munition

Some Krabs have been reported as lost in action, unsurprising as it has been in combat since June 2022 and as an SPG is a high value target for the Russians. Analysis of Russian imagery of destroyed or damaged SPGs such as the Krab indicates many of the lost weapons were left in defensive positions for extended periods. Others were being used in the same firing locations repeatedly.

Analysts studied the images, which often came from Russian UAS, and noticed the SPGs had large amounts of ammunition stacked nearby or were in well prepared positions. Staying in the same locations or using the same ones repeatedly allowed the Russians to locate and attack these guns. Mobility is a key survivability advantage of an SPG and it appears failing to use it heightens the risk to both weapon and crew.

WEAPONS OF THE UKRAINE WAR

CAESAR
French wheeled SPG

This long-range cannon's name is the French acronym for 'Camion Équipé d'un Système d'Artillerie,' which translates to 'truck mounted artillery system.' It is in the NATO-standard 155mm calibre and is equipped with an automated fire control system. The CAESAR can quickly set up, fire and move away in less than three minutes, assuming a fire mission of six rounds, which this weapon can fire in one minute.

There are several variants of the CAESAR, differentiated by the type of truck chassis used. Units purchased for the French Army use a 6x6 Renault design, but some export versions are mounted on an 8x8 Czech Tatra chassis. The most notable difference between the two is the amount of ammunition carried. The 6x6 version holds 18 rounds while the larger 8x8 has 36. Various levels of armour protection for the crew compartment are available as well.

The CAESAR saw extensive combat use before the Ukraine War. The French used them in Afghanistan, Mali and Iraq. In Iraq, French gunners employed them against the tattered remnants of the so-called Islamic State at the final Battle of Baghuz Fawqani. Other nations have used purchased CAESARs in action as well.

France and Denmark provided CAESARs to Ukraine beginning in May 2022. France transferred 30 6x6 models while Denmark gave 19 8x8 versions. The Ukrainians prize the CAESAR for its long range and ability to 'shoot and scoot' to avoid return fire. One complaint about the CAESAR and other Western systems are that control labels and manuals are often not translated into Ukrainian, making it harder for crews to learn how to operate them.

During the fighting around Adiivka in Donetsk during late 2023, the Ukrainian 55th Artillery Brigade used CAESAR howitzers with the US-produced M864 Dual Purpose Improved Conventional Munition (DPICM) round, which delivers 72 submunitions with anti-armour and anti-personnel capabilities. Such artillery fires are credited with inflicting heavy casualties among the attacking Russians.

CAESAR Self-Propelled Gun Characteristics		
Version	6x6	8x8
Origin	France	
Mass:	17,700kg (39,021lb)	Up to 30,200kg (66,579lb)
Length:	10m (32.8ft)	12.3m (40.3ft)
Crew	6 personnel	
Rate of fire:	6 rounds per minute (maximum)	
Maximum firing range	55km (31.1 miles) with rocket assisted projectile	

ABOVE: A crew from the Ukrainian 55th Artillery Brigade fires their CAESAR howitzer. The grey tube the soldier is holding is a propellant charge and the next shell can be seen in the gun's loading cradle. (UKRAINIAN MOD)

LEFT: Another view of the CAESAR firing. The ammunition storage is visible on the right side of the vehicle. The bags over the ammunition box hold camouflage netting. (UKRAINIAN MOD)

ARTILLERY

M109 series

US self-propelled gun

RIGHT: The small black dot in the upper right of this image is a 155mm shell from this Ukrainian-crewed M109 SPG. The gun laying aid on the tripod to the gun's left indicates this is an older model without integrated GPS. (US ARMY)

This howitzer entered service with the US Army in the early 1960s and first saw combat during the Vietnam War. Thanks to periodic upgrades it still serves as the primary Self-Propelled Gun (SPG) for the US Army and various versions are in service with over two dozen armies around the world. As the most common SPG in the western world, it was inevitable some would be transferred to Ukraine in its desperate need for artillery systems after the 2022 Invasion.

As of this writing over 160 M109s have been transferred to Ukraine from the United Kingdom, United States, Norway, Italy, and Latvia. Those supplied by the UK were acquired from a Belgian company. The M109 is the most numerous Western SPG in Ukrainian service.

BELOW: This M109A3GN donated by Norway is in service with the 72nd 'Black Zaporozhian' Mechanised Brigade in the Donetsk region in January 2023. (UKRAINIAN MOD)

M109 Self-Propelled Gun Characteristics	
Origin	United States
Mass:	38,101kg (84,000lb) for M109A7
Length:	9.1m (29.9ft)
Crew	4-6 personnel depending on variant
Rate of fire:	1 round per minute (sustained) 2 rounds per minute (maximum)
Maximum firing range	21km (13 miles) standard HE round 30km (18.6 miles) using rocket assisted projectile (RAP) 40km (24.8 miles) using Excalibur precision munition

Most of the Ukrainian M109s are upgraded to the 'A3' standard, which incorporated various reliability and maintenance improvements. Some have been fitted with improved fire control and navigation systems. The United States provided the M109A6 Paladin, which has armour, engine and suspension upgrades. It also has better systems for accurate gun laying and a digital communication system with encryption capability.

Unlike high-profile weapons like HIMARS and Challenger, M109s receive scant attention as they are basic gun platforms, effective but unglamorous. It is like other SPGs on the battlefield in how it functions; it reliably throws 45kg (100lb) explosive shells at the enemy. As there are thousands in existence and the M109 is still in production, spare parts and gun barrels are available, helping to keep these workhorses in the field.

A bigger problem for the M109 and similar 155mm weapons is the ammunition supply. This is a Western calibre so all supplies must come through foreign assistance. No one realised how quickly ammunition stockpiles could be depleted by modern combat. Since neither side has air superiority, artillery is the primary support weapon. Several nations are increasing production capacity to improve the ammunition flow to Ukraine and replenish existing stockpiles. The US Army is also updating its artillery doctrine to incorporate lessons from the Ukraine War.

WEAPONS OF THE UKRAINE WAR

FH-70

A towed and self-propelled cannon

The FH-70 is an example of a Western howitzer design from the late Cold War, roughly analogous to the Soviet-origin Giatsint-B. This 155mm cannon was jointly developed by three NATO nations, the United Kingdom, Germany and Italy to provide commonality and reduce development costs. Those three nations ordered about 450 of them during the late 1970s and more were purchased by other nations. Japan made the FH-70 under license.

In most respects the FH-70 is a conventional weapon typical of the era in which it was designed. However, it has one feature which is unusual for a towed artillery piece. It has a small 1.7 litre Volkswagen engine in the gun carriage. This engine helps power the gun's hydraulic system but can also move the cannon under its own power. This enables the gun to change position without a towing vehicle when necessary. With this engine the FH-70 can move up to 20km at up to 16km/h, according to Ukrainian users. In combat, this might allow the gun to be saved if its towing vehicle breaks down or is immobilised. It also might get the gun to cover before return fire arrives.

Ukraine has 34 FH-70s, 24 donated by Estonia and 10 more from Italy. It is known to be operated by the 44th Field Artillery Brigade. Ukrainian soldiers praise the FH-70 for its accuracy. One soldier of the Ukrainian 44th Artillery Brigade told Radio Free Europe, "It's so precise that the first shell lands 50-60 metres away from the target. So, the second shell hits the target. The Russians don't like it because we don't use many shells to hit a target." It is believed several FH-70s have been lost in action, however, including one struck by a Russian Lancet loitering munition.

LEFT: An FH-70 moving via its 1.7 litre Volkswagen auxiliary power unit. The driver's right hand controls a small lever which turns the rear wheels for steering and under his feet are acceleration and braking pedals. (UKRAINIAN MOD)

BELOW: Powder smoke billows from the muzzle brake of an FH-70 of the 44th Artillery Brigade after firing. This particular cannon was donated by Italy. (UKRAINIAN MOD)

FH-70 155mm Howitzer Characteristics	
Origin	United Kingdom, Germany and Italy
Mass:	9,347kg (20,606lb)
Length:	12.43m (40.8ft)
Crew	8 personnel
Rate of fire:	2 rounds per minute (sustained) 6 rounds per minute (maximum)
Maximum firing range	24.7km (15.3 miles) standard HE round 31.5km (19.5 miles) using base bleed projectile

www.keymilitary.com

ARTILLERY

DANA

Czech 152 mm wheeled SPG

RIGHT: A DANA of the 110th Brigade moves down a trail in Ukraine near Adiivka. The driver must extend outriggers to stabilise the vehicle before firing. (UKRAINIAN MOD)

Designed in then-Czechoslovakia during the 1970s, the DANA is unusual in being a wheeled SPG developed during the Cold War, when almost all artillery systems were either towed or tracked. Over 750 were built before the Cold War ended and when Czechoslovakia dissolved into the independent nations of the Czech Republic and Slovakia, the DANAs were distributed between the two countries. Hundreds more were exported, including some to the Soviet Union in the late 1980s, but those are not in service with Russia.

The DANA uses a Tatra 8x8 truck chassis mounting a large turret which holds a 152mm gun. It is equipped with an autoloader which can reload the gun at any elevation angle. This is innovative as most SPGs and even some tanks must lower their gun barrels for reloading after firing.

BELOW: The 8-wheel drive DANA has good cross-country mobility. Note the DShK 12.7mm machine gun atop the turret, used to defend against troops, light armoured vehicles and even UAS. (UKRAINIAN MOD)

The driver and section chief sit in the vehicle's front cabin while the turret holds the gunner and two ammunition handlers.

The vehicle has good ammunition capacity, 50-60 rounds, and some of the DANAs transferred to Ukraine have upgraded fire control systems. Newer versions have more powerful engines and the ability to operate with fewer crew members if needed.

Poland employed the DANA in Afghanistan and it has also seen combat in Georgia in 2008 and the Nagorno-Karabakh War in 2020.

Ukraine was considering purchasing the DANA before the 2022 invasion. The Czech Republic transferred an undisclosed number of DANAs to Ukraine in 2022.

They are issued to the 110th Mechanised Brigade, which also operates the Czech RM-70 MLRS. This unit has served much of the war around Adiivka, which saw heavy fighting in late 2023 and early 2024. Ukraine announced the DANA is also issued to the 56th Motorised Brigade and that it has received updated DANAs mounting a 155mm howitzer.

DANA 152 mm Howitzer Characteristics	
Origin	Czechoslovakia
Mass:	29,250kg (64,485lb)
Length:	11.16m (36.6ft)
Crew	5 personnel
Rate of fire:	2 rounds per minute (manual) 5 rounds per minute (semi-automatic)
Maximum firing range	20km (12.4 miles)

WEAPONS OF THE UKRAINE WAR

M777 155mm Howitzer

Lightweight American cannon system

The M777 is America's newest towed howitzer, designed to be lightweight for easy movement. The extensive use of titanium in its constructions makes the M777 7,000lbs lighter than its predecessor, the M198. The cannon can emplace in less than three minutes and after firing displaces in three minutes also. This is critical on modern battlefields where return fire can be on the way in a few minutes.

Nicknamed the 'Triple 7' by American troops, the gun has a nominal crew of eight soldiers, though five can operate it at a lower rate of fire. It can fire precision guided munitions, such as the M982 Excalibur GPS-guided round. It saw combat use in Iraq, Afghanistan and against the so-called Islamic State, so it was a battle-tested weapon by the time it arrived in Ukraine.

The United States transferred 180 M777s to Ukraine starting in April 2022. Australia gave another six and Canada four more. The US included 7,000 M982 Excalibur rounds in the delivery. Canada gave an unknown number of M982s as well. This makes the M777 the most numerous 155mm weapon system given to Ukraine. The Ukrainians state they prefer the M777 as its range matches or exceeds comparable Russian weapons.

Despite the M777's ability to be quickly displaced after firing, towed artillery is much more vulnerable to counterbattery fire or other attack. UAS are widely used in Ukraine by both sides for hunting artillery. Videos exist of Russian UAS observing M777-equipped units and then attacking them with suicide drones and artillery. While the explosions from such strikes are often dramatic, it can be hard to tell whether the target is destroyed or damaged. There is evidence about 40 M777s have been destroyed in action and about an equal number damaged.

M777 155mm Howitzer Characteristics	
Origin	United States
Mass:	4,200kg (9,300lb)
Length:	10.7m (35ft) when deployed for firing
Crew	5 to 8 personnel
Rate of fire:	2 rounds per minute (sustained) 5 rounds per minute (maximum)
Maximum barrel elevation	71.2 degrees
Maximum firing range	22.5km (14 miles) standard; 30km (19 miles) using rocket assisted projectile (RAP); 40 km (25 miles) using Excalibur guided round

ABOVE: A M777 of the Ukrainian 406th Artillery Brigade. The towing vehicle is the US M1083, the standard US truck for towing large artillery pieces. (UKRAINIAN MOD)

LEFT: An M777 crew firing their weapon. Howitzers are capable of high elevation of their gun barrels, giving their rounds an arcing trajectory. (UKRAINIAN MOD)

LEFT: This still image from drone video shows a Ukrainian M777 unit under Russian artillery attack. The danger to the gun crew is extreme. (RUSSIAN MOD)

www.keymilitary.com

AIRCRAFT

MiG-29

Supersonic fighter aircraft

ABOVE: Two Russian MiG-29Ks fly in formation with a pair or Tu-95 bombers. Fighters often escort bombers in case enemy fighters appear.
(OFFICE OF THE PRESIDENT OF THE RUSSIAN FEDERATION)

BELOW: The Ukrainians often use digital camouflage patterns on their aircraft. This MiG-29 has a solid blue underbelly to make it harder to detect from below.
(US AIR NATIONAL GUARD)

Developed during the Cold War as the Soviet counterpart to the American F-15 Eagle, the MiG-29 is in its fifth decade of service. It flies with both the Ukrainian and Russian air forces, who inherited them when the Soviet Union dissolved. The aircraft first entered service in 1983. It is generally considered to be a fourth-generation fighter, roughly on par with the F-15, F-16, or Saab Gripen, though such a comparison depends heavily upon any updates the MiG has received.

The MiG-29 is produced by the now-Russian company Mikoyan, officially known as the Russian Aircraft Corporation and often abbreviated as MiG. All aircraft made by this company bear the MiG prefix in their designation. They reportedly still produce modernised versions of the MiG-29; the name 'Fulcrum' is a NATO reporting name. Though it started as an air-to-air interceptor, updates give the Fulcrum air-to-ground strike capability.

The MiG-29 is described as simple, reliable and easy to maintain. American pilots also note that while a very manoeuvrable aircraft, it is designed to operate under the direction of a ground controller, which was a standard Soviet method but anathema to Western pilots. They rated it as less capable than similar Western fighters.

For the Russians the MiG-29 is just one aircraft type in their air fleet; they operated around 110 of them in 2022, perhaps two dozen of them MiG-29Ks in the Russian Naval Aviation service, where they served aboard Russia's single aircraft carrier, the Soviet-era Admiral Kuznetsov. That ship is in an extended refit, so some of these naval variants are flying in the Ukraine War. Some are reportedly flying with the 100th Independent Shipborne Fighter Aviation Regiment, based at Saky in Crimea.

The MiG-29 forms a major part of the Ukrainian Air Force, as they operate fewer types of aircraft and far fewer planes overall. It is estimated the Ukrainians possessed about 60 MiG-29s at the beginning of the war, operated by three fighter brigades, the 40th, 114th and 204th. Since the

WEAPONS OF THE UKRAINE WAR

war began Ukraine received more MiG-29s from Poland and Slovakia. Ukraine also had some aircraft in storage, which have been restored to flyable condition or used for parts.

This venerable aircraft has been in been in combat since 2014. Some MiG-29s, mostly in nonflying condition, were captured by Russian forces when they seized Crimea. Most or all of them were later disassembled by the Russians and sent back to Ukraine. Two Ukrainian MiG-29s were shot down in 2014 in the early stages of the Donbas fighting.

When the Russians invaded Ukraine in February 2022, MiG-29s were in combat in the first hours of the conflict. At least two were shot down by Russian interceptors while attacking the Russian helicopter air assault force moving to Antoniv Airport outside Kyiv. The Ukrainians armed the MiG-29s sent against the helicopter force with B-8M pods for the S-8 unguided 80mm rocket, apparently because their R-73 infrared homing missiles had difficulty against the low-flying helicopters. R-27 radar homing missiles were also used. The Russians lost some helicopters from this force, but the number is unknown and some were lost to shoulder-fired antiaircraft missiles.

Some MiG-29s were also lost on the ground to Russian strikes while Ukrainian pilots claimed some victories against Russian planes. Details on numbers and circumstances are scant and often cannot be confirmed. Since the beginning of the war, Ukrainians disperse their aircraft to secondary airfields and move them frequently to prevent being located by the Russians.

The Russian employ some of their MiG-29s to patrol the Black Sea area, hunting for Ukrainian naval vessels.

MiG-29 Fulcrum Characteristics	
Origin	Soviet Union
Length	17.32m (56.8ft)
Wingspan	11.36m (37.3ft)
Maximum speed	Mach 2.3 (1,764mph)
Combat radius	700-900km (434-559mi)
Service Ceiling	18,000m (59,055ft)
Armament	1 30mm cannon with 100 rounds 7 hardpoints for missiles, rockets or bombs

With far fewer planes available, the Ukrainian have armed their MiG-29s to fire the AGM-88 HARM anti-radar missile, which required modifications to the aircraft. Ukrainian MiG-29s can also drop JDAM bombs. Conscious of losses, Ukrainian MiG-29s coordinate with S-300 missile batteries and other air defences as part of an integrated network. They are reportedly effective at shooting down Shahed UAS (page 95) with their 30mm cannon.

ABOVE: For every hour a combat aircraft spends in the sky, hours are spent in maintenance. This MiG-29 in a hanger is armed with a pair of R-73 infrared homing missiles and an R-27 radar homing missile. (UKRAINIAN MOD)

BELOW: This MiG-29 was reportedly refurbished to flying condition and painted in a silver, grey and white digital pattern. Note the R-27 radar homing missile on its wing pylon. (UKRAINIAN MOD)

AIRCRAFT

MiG-31

Russian high-altitude interceptor

ABOVE: At least ten MiG-31s were modified into the K variant, which carries the Kinzhal missile. They frequently take part in Russian missile attacks on Ukrainian infrastructure and industry. (RUSSIAN MOD)

RIGHT: Two MiG-31s at altitude. The aircraft resembles its predecessor, the MiG-25. Despite the dissolution of the Soviet Union, the Russian Air Force still uses the red star for identification. (RUSSIAN AIR FORCE)

The Soviet Union developed the MiG-31 (*Foxhound* is the NATO reporting name) in the late 1970s to replace the famed MiG-25 *Foxbat*. Only the Russian and Kazakh air forces operate it and the Kazakh planes are older production units inherited when the Soviet Union collapsed.

The MiG-31 is a large, twin-engine aircraft equipped with a 'look down/shoot down' radar. This allows the MiG-31 to engage low flying cruise missiles and aircraft. The radar in upgraded MiG-31s can detect fighters at up to 200 km and track up to 24 targets. The MiG also has some ability to communicate with other airborne and ground based sensors and share location and targeting information.

The Russian Air Force uses the MiG-31 in two roles. The MiG-31K variant is modified to carry the Kinzhal missile (see page 105). The aircraft's combat range combined with the missile's own range allow Kinzhals to be launched outside Ukraine's air defence zone. This means the aircraft can fire and return to its base without being exposed to enemy fire, leaving Ukrainian defences to deal with the missile.

The MiG-31 has also proven successful in its original role as a high-altitude interceptor. The aircraft can operate at 50-60,000 feet, above the altitude at which Ukrainian forces are able to effectively engage. Using its radar to target lower flying Ukrainian units, the MiG-31 uses the R-37 missile, which has a range of 200 miles and was designed to hit distant targets, though it is reportedly most effective within 80 miles.

The missiles available to Ukrainian pilots have ranges of up to 50 miles. This allows the MiG-31 pilots to avoid any return fire, particularly as the R-37 is a fire and forget missile, so the Russian flyers can turn away since they do not need to maintain target lock on their opponents. MiG-31 pilots are believed to have had good success against Ukrainian aircraft using this tactic. Ukrainian pilots state the MiG-31 has only downed a few aircraft this way, but such attacks more often force Ukrainian pilots to abort their mission, which accomplishes the Russian goal as well.

MiG-31 Foxhound Characteristics	
Origin	Soviet Union
Length	22.62m (74.2ft)
Wingspan	13.45m (44.1ft)
Maximum speed	Mach 2.83 (1,764 mph) at 21,500 m
Combat radius	720-1450km (447-900mi)
Service Ceiling	25,000m (82020ft)
Armament	23mm cannon with 800 rounds 8 hardpoints for missiles

WEAPONS OF THE UKRAINE WAR

Su-27

Air superiority fighter

Su-27 Flanker Characteristics	
Origin	Soviet Union
Length	21.9m (71.8ft)
Wingspan	14.7m (48.2ft)
Maximum speed	Mach 2.35 (1803mph)
Combat radius	1340km (832mi)
Service Ceiling	19,000m (62,335ft)
Armament	30mm cannon with 150 rounds 10 hardpoints for missiles, bombs and rockets

Designed by the Soviet Union as a counter to the US F-15 Eagle, the Su-27 in a twin-engine, single seat fighter originally designed for combat against enemy fighters. Subsequent upgrades have given it the ability to perform air to ground missions as well. It is flown by both Russia and Ukraine. The Su-27 is known for its manoeuvrability and for many years was shown off at air shows doing the "cobra' manoeuvre, where the pilot pitches the nose up and skids the aircraft forward on its tail before recovering.

Estimates on how many Su-27s are flying with each air force vary. The Russian Air Force may have as many as 390, with varying ideas as to how many are serviceable. Given their access to the manufacturer for spare parts and maintenance, it is likely a high percentage are flying.

Ukraine inherited 70-75 Su-27s when the Soviet Union dissolved, so these are older models which have not benefitted from more recent upgrade programs. Many of these were in storage until 2014, when the seizure of Crimea and the Donbass War brought increased defence spending in Ukraine. Before 2014, Ukraine had perhaps two dozen in service; now the number is around 50, not including losses, which may be over a dozen aircraft.

Russian losses of the Su-27 are unknown. Notably, In March 2023 a Russian Su-27 downed an American MQ9 drone over the Black Sea by dumping fuel onto it and then colliding with it. The Ukrainian Air Force is cautious with its Su-27s, as there are no sources for replacement aircraft abroad, as with the MiG-29 or Su-25. They don't have access to a spare parts pipeline, so some aircraft have probably been cannibalised to keep others flying. Like other Ukrainian combat aircraft, the Su-27s are moved frequently to make them harder targets for Russian attack. They have received some homegrown upgrades and have been equipped with Western ordnance. Ukrainian Su-27s have been seen carrying the US-made AGM88 HARM missile and JDAM precision guided bomb.

LEFT: This worn-looking but well-armed Russian fighter carries four R-27 and two R-73 missiles. The Su-27 is dangerous in a dogfight but is more vulnerable against advanced fighters which can engage beyond visual range. (UK MOD/CROWN COPYRIGHT)

BELOW: This Ukrainian Su-27 carries a pair of R-27 radar homing missiles on its under-fuselage pylons and one R-73 infrared homing (heat-seeking) missile on a wing pylon. (USAF)

AIRCRAFT

SU-34

Russian strike aircraft

The Sukhoi Su-34 appeared shortly before the Soviet Union dissolved. However, it suffered development setbacks due to budget shortfalls and didn't enter service with the Russian Air Force until 2014. The Su-34 is a large, all-weather, twin-engine fighter-bomber with a crew of two and good ground attack capabilities. It is distinguished by the small canards on the fuselage forward of the wings. The shape of its cockpit and nose area have earned it the nickname 'hellduck.'

The aircraft is well-armed, carrying a 30mm cannon and hardpoints to carry a variety of weapons. This includes unguided bombs, air to air missiles, ground attack missiles, cruise missiles, rocket pods, anti-radiation (radar) missiles and even anti-ship missiles. The crew of two sit side-by-side in a large cockpit which actually has a small heating unit for canned food and a toilet for long distance flights. Production is ongoing and the Russians are believed to have acquired about 150 of them but have lost over two dozen during the War in Ukraine.

This loss rate is largely due to the SU-34's primary role as a ground attack aircraft. Such missions naturally bring it within range of Ukrainian air defences, from MANPADS to S-300 and Patriot surface to air missile launchers. It is riskier when the SU-34 is carrying unguided bombs, as it must fly lower to ensure greater accuracy. When using precision guided weapons, the aircraft can fly higher, staying out of range of the low-level air defence systems.

Despite these losses, the SU-34 is an effective strike aircraft and is also believed capable of carrying electronic warfare and reconnaissance pods, giving it multi-mission capability. Its ability to carry a wide range of missiles allows it to carry out tactical missions over the battlefield or strategic-level sorties such as missile attacks against Ukrainian industry and infrastructure.

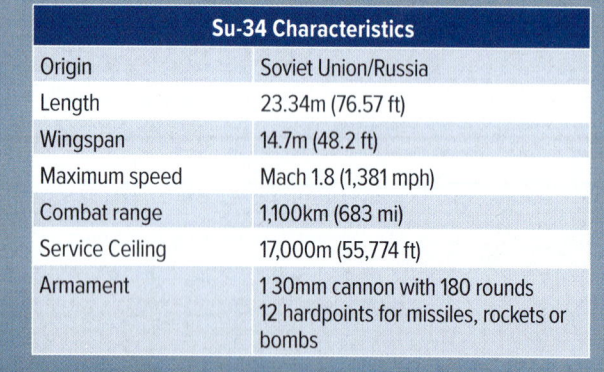

RIGHT: The size of the Su-34 is apparent in this image, with the pilot visible in the right side of the cockpit. This aircraft has its refuelling probe extended. (RUSSIAN MOD)

BELOW: This Su-34 is taking off for a bombing mission in March 2022. Note the aircraft's number is obscured for security reasons. It appears to be carrying four bombs. (RUSSIAN MOD)

Su-34 Characteristics	
Origin	Soviet Union/Russia
Length	23.34m (76.57 ft)
Wingspan	14.7m (48.2 ft)
Maximum speed	Mach 1.8 (1,381 mph)
Combat range	1,100km (683 mi)
Service Ceiling	17,000m (55,774 ft)
Armament	1 30mm cannon with 180 rounds 12 hardpoints for missiles, rockets or bombs

80 WEAPONS OF THE UKRAINE WAR

WEAPONS OF THE UKRAINE WAR

SU-25

Rugged ground attack aircraft

Frequently known by its NATO reporting name '*Frogfoot*,' the Su-25 is a twin-engine single seat jet aircraft optimised for ground attack. Aircraft specially designed for ground attack are often generically called 'Shturmoviks,' partly in reference to the famous Soviet Ilyushin Il-2 ground attack plane of World War II. The Su-25 entered service in the Soviet Union in 1981 and is often compared to the USAF's A-10 Thunderbolt II as they are similar in purpose.

Su-25s are armoured to protect the pilot and vital areas of the aircraft from ground fire. They are also manoeuvrable and can carry a wide variety of gun pods, bombs, unguided rockets and air to surface missiles. They are also able to carry air to air infrared homing missiles for self-defence against fighters or to attack enemy helicopters. Su-25s also carry chaff and flare dispensers to ward off incoming missiles.

Russia had about 190 Su-25s in service when the war began, while Ukraine had around 30 flying, with another 12 in storage but considered flyable. It appears both sides have lost about 50 Su-25s altogether so far. It is unknown how many Russia might have in storage. The Ukrainians have been able to make good most of their losses through transfers of 18 Su-25s from other nations, such as Bulgaria and North Macedonia. Some of these aircraft may not have been flyable and could be restored or used for spare parts.

Workhorse aircraft such as the Su-25 perform important but unglamorous work and are seldom mentioned in media reporting, except when they are reported as shot down. Several have been reported as downed by MANPADS. Ukraine regularly disperses its aircraft to reduce the threat of destruction by Russian missiles. A video released by Russia shows a Ukrainian Su-25 being struck and set aflame by a Lancet loitering munition in October 2023.

Su-25 Grach Characteristics	
Origin	Soviet Union
Length	15.53 m (50.95 ft)
Wingspan	14.36 m (47.1 ft)
Maximum speed	975 km/h (605 mph)
Combat radius	750 km (466 mi)
Service Ceiling	7,000 m (22,965 ft)
Armament	30mm cannon with 250 rounds 11 hardpoints for missiles, gun pods, bombs and rockets

ABOVE: A group of Ukrainian pilots in front of an Su-25. The aircraft's compact and rugged frame make it resistant to ground fire. (UKRAINIAN MOD)

LEFT: The slow, low-flying Su-25 is a good platform for launching accurate barrages with rocket pods or to strafe with gun pods. (BULGARIAN MOD)

www.keymilitary.com

AIRCRAFT

Mi-8/Mi-17 Hip

Versatile utility helicopter

RIGHT: The Russian Army uses the Mi-8 for its VDV airborne and air assault troops; an Mi-8 can carry an impressive 24 troops. (RUSSIAN MOD)

The Mil Mi-8 helicopter, NATO reporting name '*Hip*,' is among the most widely used helicopters in the world, in service with over 80 nations. A modernised version, known in Russia as the Mi-8M, is widely known by its export name, Mi-17, elsewhere. A simple way to differentiate the two models is by the tail rotor; the Mi-8's is on the starboard side while the Mi-17's is on the left. Mi-8s have been flying since the 1960s and will continue to do so for decades more.

They are mainly used in the transport and cargo roles but can also be equipped as gunships, able to carry 4,000 kg of cargo or weapons or up to 24 personnel. Their rugged, simple design makes them easy to maintain even under austere battlefield conditions. There are numerous variants including command and control, minelaying, reconnaissance, aerial ambulance and electronic warfare.

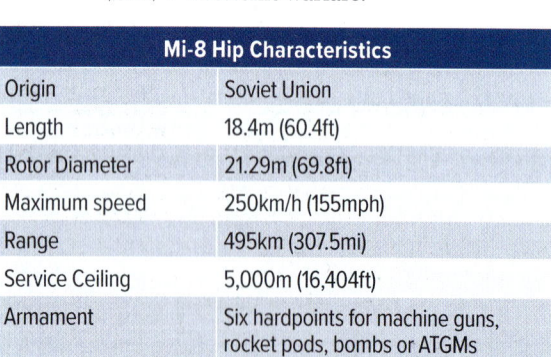

BELOW: Medical evacuation is a vital role for helicopters on the battlefield; an infantry soldier's morale is boosted by the knowledge medical treatment is a possibility. (US ARMY)

Mi-8 Hip Characteristics	
Origin	Soviet Union
Length	18.4m (60.4ft)
Rotor Diameter	21.29m (69.8ft)
Maximum speed	250km/h (155mph)
Range	495km (307.5mi)
Service Ceiling	5,000m (16,404ft)
Armament	Six hardpoints for machine guns, rocket pods, bombs or ATGMs

The Mi-8 is the primary utility helicopter of both air forces. The Russian operated over 700 while the Ukrainian count varies from 40 to around 100. Mi-17s were transferred to Ukraine as part of the international aid effort. Sixteen of these Mi-17s were originally acquired by the United States for Afghanistan as part of a military aid program to that nation. When the Afghan government fell and that nation was taken over by the Taliban, the US kept the helicopters as it had paid for them. Eleven were in storage in the US while five were actually already in Ukraine undergoing maintenance.

Early in the war, Mi-8s were used to resupply Ukrainian forces in the Azovstal steel plant during the fighting in Mariupol from February to May 2022. Several were shot down in the effort.

A notable incident involved a Russian pilot who defected to Ukraine with his Mi-8 helicopter in August 2023. Ukrainian intelligence reportedly spent six months working to convince the pilot to come over with his aircraft. The aircraft was carrying a load of spare parts for the Su-27 fighter, which Ukraine also operates. The pilot went to live in Spain and was murdered in early 2024.

WEAPONS OF THE UKRAINE WAR

Ka-52

Russian attack helicopter

The Ka-52 is a two-seat version of the single seat Ka-50. It began development during the 1980s in the Soviet Union and was finished by Russia. The Ka-50 entered service in 1995, but few were produced due to Russia's post-Cold War economic difficulties. The Ka-52 entered service in 2011.

Unusually, the Ka-52 has no tail rotor, as it has coaxial main rotors, one above the other. This gives the helicopter more power for the main rotors and allows it to keep flying even if the tail is damaged. There are reports of Ka-52s continuing to fly even with the tail shot off. It has ejection seats for the crew. In the event of an ejection the rotor blades detach via explosive bolts, to avoid striking the crew as they leave the aircraft.

The 30 mm cannon fires a selection of ammunition including armour-piercing, explosive, or fragmentation rounds, selectable by the pilot. The fire control system can share and receive information from other helicopters or a ground reconnaissance team for coordinated attacks. The Ka-52 can carry several different kinds of laser guided anti-tank missiles or the LMUR missile, which has a 14.5 km range.

Ka-50s saw combat in Chechnya while Ka-52s saw action in Syria, where they proved effective gunships. The Ka-52 entered combat in Ukraine as soon as the 2022 war began. They flew escort for the Russian VDV heliborne assault force which seized Antonov Airport outside Kyiv on 24 February 2022. These helicopters traded fire with Ukrainian troops along the ingress route and then provided fire support at the airport.

In the first weeks of the war, Russian attack helicopters flew deep patrols behind Ukrainian lines, hunting for targets. As Ukrainian troops received more MANPADS they began to shoot down more Russian helicopters. Afterward Russian pilots became more cautious, staying closer to their own lines to reduce the anti-air threat. There is evidence one or two Ka-52s were shot down using the Stugna-P anti-tank missile. This is feasible if the helicopter is hovering or moving slowly.

Ka-52 Alligator Characteristics	
Origin	Soviet Union/Russia
Length	16m (52.5ft)
Rotor Diameter	14.5m (47.5ft)
Maximum speed	300km/h (186mph)
Range	460km (285mi)
Service Ceiling	5,500m (18,044ft)
Armament	30-mm cannon with 460 rounds 6 hardpoints for ordnance, ranging from gun pods, unguided rocket pods, bombs, anti-armour missiles and air to air missiles

ABOVE: Taken from video released by the Russian military, these frames show a Ka-52 attacking Ukrainian positions at the Antonov airport near Kyiv on 24 February 2022. The video shows the pilots firing unguided rockets and the 30mm cannon. (RUSSIAN MOD)

LEFT: A Ka-52 near Kharkiv in April 2022. Note the retracted landing gear, front sensor pod and the missiles, rocket pod and fuel tank on its stub wings. (RUSSIAN MOD)

AIRCRAFT

Mi-24

Classic Soviet-era attack helicopter

The Mi-24, often known by its NATO reporting name *Hind*, is a large attack helicopter dating from the early 1970s. This robust Soviet design is prized for its ruggedness and has served in the militaries of over 50 nations worldwide. It is the primary attack helicopter of the Ukrainian military and is still in service with the Russian military alongside two newer attack helicopters. The Ukrainians operated around 35 in 2022 and have acquired another 28 from foreign assistance. The Russians are believed to have over 300 in service. These numbers do not account for any losses.

Hinds carry an impressive payload of rockets, missiles and guns, providing firepower to support ground troops. Its crews refer to it as the 'flying tank' for good reason. This heavy ordnance load allows the Mi-24 to loiter on the battlefield and provide fire support to troops on the ground or hunt for targets. Unique among attack helicopter designs, the Mi-24 has a crew compartment which can also carry up to eight troops if needed.

The age of the helicopter does provide maintenance and operational challenges; Ukraine's Mi-24s are older than most of the pilots flying it and it is likely the same for the Russians. Ukrainian pilots report they often fly three or four sorties a day and must be careful to avoid Russian air defences. In November 2023, Ukraine released video showing a *Hind*-G1 in flight. This rare Cold War variant is designed to conduct reconnaissance of nuclear battlefields, measuring radiation levels. Short of attack helicopters, Ukraine likely reactivated it for the gunship role.

Mi-24s are workhorse helicopters, flying important but unglamorous air support missions. The model's most famous mission so far came on 1 April 2022 when two Ukrainian Mi-24s crossed the border into Russia and attack a fuel storage depot in Belgorod. They fired unguided S-8 rockets at the fuel storage tanks, igniting at least eight or them. Though the Ukrainian government did not take credit for the mission at the time, it is assumed they flew a daring cross border raid.

Mi-24 Hind Characteristics	
Origin	Soviet Union
Length	17.5m (57.4ft)
Rotor Diameter	17.3m (56.8ft)
Maximum speed	335km/h (208mph)
Range	450km (279.6mi)
Service Ceiling	4,900m (16,076ft)
Armament	12.7-, 23-, or 30-mm cannon depending on variant 1500 kg of ordnance, ranging from gun pods, unguided rocket pods, mine dispensers, bombs, anti-armour missiles and air to air missiles

BELOW: Mi-24s can lay down massive barrages of unguided rockets, seen here during an exercise in 2017. (RUSSIAN MOD)

BOTTOM: This Ukrainian Mi-24 is making an impressive firepower display using rocket and cannon fire. (UKRAINIAN MOD)

84 WEAPONS OF THE UKRAINE WAR

WEAPONS OF THE UKRAINE WAR

Mi-28 Havoc

Advanced Russian attack helicopter

Like the Ka-52, the Mi-28 began development in the Soviet Union during the 1980s, which was continued by Russia in the 1990s. Several pauses occurred due to lack of funding, but over time the helicopter was completed and delivered to the military in 2006. Russia has somewhere around 100 in service and production is ongoing. Mi-28s saw prior combat in Syria.

Originally designed as an anti-armour platform carrying up to 16 ATGM, the Mi-28 evolved into a versatile weapon able to use a variety of missiles and rockets along with its 30mm cannon. Like many modern attack helicopters, it can also carry air-to-air infrared homing missiles for use against aircraft. The cockpit is armoured to withstand up to 14.5mm bullets. It has a small compartment able to carry up to three people and is intended for picking up the crews of downed aircraft rather than transporting troops.

The Mi-28 has suffered proportionately fewer losses in Ukraine compared to the Ka-52. In part this is due to the Ka-52's need to hover while engaging targets with its laser guided weapons, which makes it more vulnerable to enemy fire. The Ka-52 also lacks countermeasures against radar guided missiles, though it does possess them against laser and infrared guided missiles. The Mi-28 has countermeasures against radar guided missiles.

The Russians pair Mi-28s with Ka-52s as each has countermeasures against different weapons, so the helicopters can protect each other when attacked, no matter what kind of guidance the incoming missile uses. Mi-28s can protect Ka-52s when they must hover to use their laser guided weapons.

Mi-28s are also used to engage drones both on the battlefield and against the longer ranged drones Ukraine launches against target inside Russian territory. Some Mi28s appear to be assigned along the Russian border specifically for this duty.

ABOVE: This Mi-28 carries the famous Russian 'Z' symbol during a mission in Ukraine in March 2022. Note a censor has obscured the helicopter's numbers on the fuselage and tail. (RUSSIAN MOD)

Mi-28 Havoc Characteristics	
Origin	Soviet Union/Russia
Length	17.01m (55.8ft)
Rotor Diameter	17.2m (56.4ft)
Maximum speed	320km/h (198mph)
Range	435km (270mi)
Service Ceiling	5,700m (18,700ft)
Armament	30mm cannon with 250 rounds 4 hardpoints for ordnance, ranging from gun pods, unguided rocket pods, bombs, anti-armour missiles and air to air missiles

LEFT: An Mi-28 returns from a mission in Ukraine, firing ATGM at Ukrainian positions in 2022. Note the empty missile racks on the helicopters left outer pylon. (RUSSIAN MOD)

www.keymilitary.com

ANTI-AIRCRAFT WEAPONS

ZU-23-2

A versatile anti-aircraft cannon

RIGHT: ZU-23-2s are emplaced around Kyiv and other population centres and infrastructure sites to defend against drone attacks.
(UKRAINIAN NATIONAL GUARD)

BELOW: These Ukrainian troops are practicing with their ZU-23-2s, one ground-mounted and the other atop an MT-LB APC. This Cold War weapon is most effective against ground targets and slower, low-flying aircraft and UAS.
(UKRAINIAN MOD)

The ZU-23-2 is a Cold War-era Soviet-designed anti-aircraft cannon system using a pair of 2A14 23mm automatic cannon. It is one of the most widely used anti-aircraft weapons in the world, as the Soviets produced over 100,000 of them and distributed them widely as military aid. In addition, the weapon has also been made under license in Bulgaria, Egypt, Poland and China.

It is mounted on a small trailer which also serves as the firing platform by moving the wheels to enable the trailer to sit on the ground. The two-soldier crew sits on small seats attached to the weapon and use either an optical-mechanical sight against aircraft or a simpler optical sight against ground targets. Each cannon is fed by an ammunition box holding a 50-round belt. A fully equipped system has a spare barrel for each gun, which should be changed after 100 rounds to avoid overheating.

Both Russian and Ukrainian forces use the ZU-23-2. While it is an older design with limited effectiveness against modern jet aircraft, it can still be effective against unarmoured helicopters and is deadly against infantry. Lightly armoured vehicles and trucks are also vulnerable. Russian troops are said to use the nick-name 'Sergei' for the weapon.

Because the ZU-23-2 is relatively lightweight, it is frequently mounted on vehicles to improves it mobility or to create an improvised fighting vehicle. In Ukraine, it has been seen mounted in the beds of lorries and on MT-LB and BTR-ZD personnel carriers. In October 2023 the Russians were seen mounting them on the back of a BMP-1 IFV, behind the vehicle's existing turret. The Ukrainians are putting them to use against Russian UAS as they are a relatively economical means of downing small, inexpensive drones.

ZU-23-2 Anti-aircraft Cannon	
Caliber	23mm
Rate of fire	2,000 rounds per minute
Effective Range	2 – 2.5km (1.25 – 1.55 miles)
Effective altitude	2,000m (6.562 ft)
Length	4.57m (15ft)
Weight	.95 tonnes (2,094lbs)
Origin	Soviet Union, 1960

86 WEAPONS OF THE UKRAINE WAR

WEAPONS OF THE UKRAINE WAR

2K22 Tunguska

Self-propelled air defence system

The Soviet Union designed the 2K22 as a replacement for the venerable ZSU-23-4 Shilka, which is actually still in wide service as well. Development took place in the 1970s, partly as a response to new NATO designs such as the A-10 Thunderbolt close support aircraft and AH-64 attack helicopter.

These Western designs were armoured to resist the 23mm cannon rounds of the Shilka, so the Tunguska was given a pair of larger 30mm cannon to give it more punch. The 30mm also has a longer range, allowing it to engage higher flying targets. The Tunguska has even greater engagement capabilities because it is also equipped with eight 9M311 surface to air missiles. There is one cannon on each side of the turret with four missile launchers beneath each cannon. Older versions of the Tunguska have two missiles under each gun.

A target acquisition radar is mounted on the turret. This radar detects targets as high as 3,500m and as distant as 18km. This is sufficient for a battlefield air defence system designed to engage helicopters, low flying aircraft and missiles during their low altitude approaches.

The Russian military operates a modernized version with the ability to engage cruise missiles. It also uses improved, longer ranged missiles and has better target tracking electronics and better fire control. A Tunguska battery typically has six 2K22s, supported by command, ammunition and maintenance vehicles. A fully equipped air defence platoon in a Russian BTG has a pair of Tunguskas with 2 9A34M2 Strela-10 anti-aircraft missile launchers.

Both the Ukrainian and Russian militaries operate the Tunguska. The missiles are effective against higher flying targets while the 30mm cannon, while can go into action more quickly, can be devastating against low flying helicopters and planes. The cannon is also effective against ground targets due to its high-explosive shells and high rate of fire.

2K22 Tunguska Air Defence System	
Origin	Soviet Union
Length	7.9m (25.9ft)
Mass	35,000kg (77,161lb)
Armament	2 30mm cannon with 1,900 rounds 8 9M311 surface to air missiles
Rate of Fire	Up to 2,500 rounds per minute per gun
Maximum range	4km (2.48mi) for cannon 10km (6.21ft) for missiles
Ceiling	2,000m (6,561ft) for cannon 3,500m (11,482ft) for missiles

ABOVE: A Ukrainian Tunguska firing a cannon burst during the Donbass War in 2015. Note the large number of casings being ejected from the rear of the vehicle. (UKRAINIAN MOD)

LEFT: This Tunguska of the Ukrainian 30th Mechanised Brigade has its radar folded down in travel position and some improvised camouflage, which is of little use in the open but can help when hiding in a tree line. (UKRAINIAN MOD)

www.keymilitary.com

ANTI-AIRCRAFT SYSTEMS

Pantsir

Russian gun/missile air defence platform

RIGHT: Ukrainian militia examine an abandoned Russian Pantsir in this image taken from video. Note the Ukrainian climbing out of the vehicle's rear compartment, their head barely visible near the door. (UKRAINIAN MINISTRY OF INTERNAL AFFAIRS)

BELOW: Two Pantsir air defence vehicles, showing their radars and missile tubes. The UK Ministry of Defence stated the Russians are taking Pantsirs from the Kaliningrad military enclave to replace battlefield losses. (RUSSIAN MOD)

The Pantsir is a capable air defence system which began development shortly before the dissolution of the Soviet Union and was finished by Russia. It is intended to supersede the Tunguska system and, on the surface, appears to be a wheeled version of its predecessor. However, the Pantsir incorporates a number of improvements.

The Pantsir's weapons load includes a pair of 30mm cannon. These weapons can fire high explosive, fragmentation or armour piercing ammunition as selected by the gunner. It also carries twelve 57E6 surface to air missiles, each in its own launch tube. It can fire either weapon type while moving and can engage ground targets.

The fire control system uses radar or a thermal imager to detect and track targets and guides its missiles using a radio link. The system can track up to 20 targets and fire at four simultaneously. A Pantsir can operate individually but usually work in batteries of six vehicles with command and resupply vehicles.

Pantsir is operated by the Russian military; Ukraine captured a few examples early in the war, but none appear to be currently in use. Pantsir units are often linked in with larger surface to air missile systems such as the S-300 and S-400 as part of an integrated air defence network. The Pantsir is also used frequently to protect the larger SAM units from incoming aerial threats.

Ukraine launches occasional UAS strikes into Russia, typically against command and control, headquarters and air bases operating bombers and fighters used against Ukrainian targets. Several Pantsir vehicles are emplaced in Moscow, sometimes on the roofs of buildings, to defend against those attacks. Russian officials have reported shooting down several UAS using the Pantsir in concert with electronic warfare systems. The Pantsir is effective against aircraft, helicopters, UAS and some missiles.

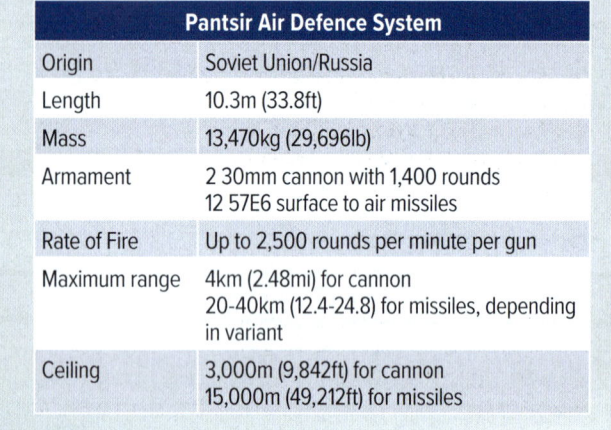

Pantsir Air Defence System	
Origin	Soviet Union/Russia
Length	10.3m (33.8ft)
Mass	13,470kg (29,696lb)
Armament	2 30mm cannon with 1,400 rounds 12 57E6 surface to air missiles
Rate of Fire	Up to 2,500 rounds per minute per gun
Maximum range	4km (2.48mi) for cannon 20-40km (12.4-24.8) for missiles, depending in variant
Ceiling	3,000m (9,842ft) for cannon 15,000m (49,212ft) for missiles

Tor

Russian short-range air defence

Tor Air Defence System	
Origin	Soviet Union/Russia
Length	7.5m (24.6ft)
Mass	34,000kg (74,957lb)
Armament	8 9M330 or 16 9M338 missiles
Maximum range	15km (9.32mi) with 9M330 missile 16km (9.94mi) with 9M338 missile
Ceiling	6km (19,685ft) with 9M330 missile 12km (39,370ft) with 9M338 missile

LEFT: A trio of Tor-M2s of the Russian 538th Guards Anti-Aircraft Missile Regiment move down a muddy track. This is the air defence units for the 4th Guards Tank Division, which began the war fighting around Kharkiv. (RUSSIAN MOD)

The 9K330 Tor is a tracked, self-propelled air defence missile system. Development began in the 1980s and it entered service in 1991. The Tor has been upgraded several times during its service to keep it competitive against evolving aerial threats.

Tor is designed to defend against aircraft, helicopters, precision munitions and missiles. The original concept placed particular focus on defending against cruise missiles like the US Tomahawk, which were a new threat in the 1980s. Battlefield experience in Ukraine shows it is also effective against UAS.

Two radars provide surveillance and tracking of up to 48 targets. These radars are designed to be resistant to jamming and can effectively detect objects with small radar cross sections, such as cruise missiles and small UAS. The radar has a range of 25km and the Tor has an optical tracking system with 20km range as a backup.

The Tor carries eight 9M330 missiles as its basic load, mounted in vertical launch tubes atop its turret. The latest upgrade to the system enables the use of new 9M338 missiles, which have a slightly longer range, can reach targets at a higher ceiling and the ability to detect targets out to 32km. Combat load for the 9M338 is 16 missiles. Tors are able to detect and track targets while moving and the newer versions have a limited ability to fire while moving.

Though not linked to the Ukraine War, an Iranian Tor shot down a Ukrainian airliner in 2020. Iran stated the incident was an accident caused by human error, possible due to fears of an Israeli air strike at the time. The Russian military uses the Tor both on the battlefield and to protect critical sites from Ukrainian cross-border attacks. Tors apparently protect Moscow alongside the Pantsir and other air defence systems. The UK Government stated the Tor system has proven effective in Russian service in Ukraine.

In one strange incident, in September 2022 Ukrainian police arrested two citizens for hiding an abandoned Russian Tor system along with an unknown number of missiles. The police turned the missiles over to the army.

LEFT: The Tor's large turret contains its two radar systems and the roof-mounted vertical launch tubes for its missiles. (RUSSIAN MOD)

ANTI-AIRCRAFT WEAPONS

S-300
Cold War surface to air missile

ABOVE: S-300s are designed for mobile operations and can use either wheeled or tracked vehicles. The system is optimised for protecting infrastructure and population centres.
(RUSSIAN MOD)

RIGHT: Fully deployed S-300 units spread their launchers out to minimise the effect of any incoming enemy fire. The weapon launches vertically so the launcher does not need to turn to face a target.
(RUSSIAN MOD)

The S-300 entered service in the Soviet Union in 1978 and has been periodically upgraded since to improve its effectiveness against cruise and ballistic missiles. The Soviet Union distributed the system widely across the Warsaw Pact and other client states. Several nations aligned to Russia, such as China, Venezuela and Iran also use the system.

As a former Soviet state, Ukraine also operates the S-300, having inherited a number of them. Only a few were in service when the Russians invaded Crimea in 2014, causing the Ukrainians to begin refurbishing S-300 systems in storage. Slovakia gifted an S-300 battery it retained from its Warsaw Pact days.

S-300 is the designation for the entire system, including launchers, radars and missiles, all of which have their own sub-designation. See the table for information on various versions of the missiles.

The Russian have built inflatable versions of the S-300 system as decoys. These decoys contain equipment which replicates the weapon's electromagnetic signature. During the Ukraine War the Russians have also used the S-300 against ground targets. This is a little-known capability of the weapon and a Ukrainian official stated the repurposed missiles are equipped with GPS receivers but are still inaccurate.

The Ukrainians have devised a way to use their older S-200 systems for ground attack as well, reserving their S300s for air defence. It is believed the Russians are using S-300s to bolster their dwindling supplies of more modern missiles. Speaking on the matter in 2022, Sir Jeremy Fleming, then head of the UK's intelligence agency GCHQ, stated, "We know – and Russian commanders on the ground know – that their supplies and munitions are running out." However, this problem applies to both sides, particularly for older missile types no longer in production.

S-300 Missile Characteristics

Missile	5V-55R	48N6	48N6DM	40N6
Production date	1981	1990	2011	2018
Length (m)	7.25m	7.25m	7.5m	7.5m
Warhead weight (kg)	130	143	180	180
Range vs. aircraft (km)	75	150	250	380
Range vs. Missile (km)	N/A	N/A	60	150
Maximum Altitude (km)	5	27	30	40
Maximum Speed (m/sec)	1,200	2,800	4,800	4,800

WEAPONS OF THE UKRAINE WAR

Patriot

US-built surface to air missile

The United States designed the Patriot missile system in the 1970s and 1980s to be the US Army's primary medium-range Surface to Air Missile (SAM) system. Patriot is actually an acronym for the system's radar, 'Phased Array Tracking Radar to Intercept on Target.' It entered service in 1984 and has been periodically upgraded since. Including Ukraine, 18 nations employ the Patriot, making it one of the more widely used Western SAMs.

Initially intended as an anti-aircraft weapon, upgraded Patriot missiles are effective against UAS, loitering munitions, ballistic and cruise missiles. Upgraded versions go by the acronym PAC (Patriot Advanced Capability). The basic system is also called the MIM-104 (Mobile Interceptor Missile 104). PAC-1 and -2 missiles give varying levels of capability against ballistic missiles, while the PAC-3 is substantially redesigned to make it more effective against ballistic missiles. It provides a hit-to-kill ability, where it destroys the incoming target by physically striking it.

A Patriot battery typically consists of a radar, control station, generator vehicle, support and ammunition trucks and six to eight launchers, each of which carries four to 16 missiles, depending on type. The most modern systems can only fire the PAC-2 or PAC-3 missiles. Launchers can be sited up to 10km from the radar, increasing the area a battery can defend.

Germany donated two complete Patriot batteries with two extra launchers while the US gave one battery with two extra launchers donated by the Netherlands. In January 2024 NATO announced the purchase of 1,000 Patriot missiles to reinforce Ukraine and bolster its own defences.

The Patriot has proven effective in the skies over Ukraine. On 4th May 2023, Ukraine reported intercepting a Russian Kinzhal over Kyiv and two weeks later claimed the intercept of six more Kinzhals in one engagement. A Patriot battery was damaged during the attack. One Ukrainian air defence officer credited Patriot with saving thousands of civilian lives due to its effectiveness against ballistic missiles. It has been credited with downing Russian tactical aircraft.

On 20th February 2024, the Russian military claimed to have intercepted a Patriot using an unspecified system, but this has not been confirmed.

MIM-104 Patriot Missile System Characteristics	
Country of Origin	United States
Maximum Range	105km (65.2mi) MIM-104A 160km (99.4mi) MIM-104D/E PAC 2 80km (49.7mi) MIM-104F PAC-3 (Aircraft target) 40km (24.8mi) MIM-104F PAC-3 (Ballistic missile target)
Maximum Firing Altitude	18.3km (11.3mi) MIM-104A 32km (19.8mi) MIM-104D/E PAC 2 24km (14.9mi) MIM-104F PAC-3 (Aircraft target) 20km (12.4mi) MIM-104F PAC-3 (Ballistic missile target)
Missiles	4 per launcher, 8 launchers in a battery

LEFT: This Patriot battery is set up in a secure fenced area for training exercise. In action air defence batteries are normally spread apart, often by kilometres, to reduce losses if attacked and defend a larger area. (US ARMY)

BELOW: A PAC-2 missile races from its launcher with a cloud of smoke and flame. While not as advanced as the PAC-3, this missile provides a good blend of capability against aircraft, ballistic and cruise missiles. (US ARMY)

ANTI-AIRCRAFT SYSTEMS

NASAMS

Norwegian/American air defence system

RIGHT: NASAMS batteries are networked to each other and other air defence systems, allowing them to coordinate fire against large air attacks. (KONGSBERG AEROSPACE AND DEFENCE)

Development of the Norwegian Advanced Surface to Air Missile System (NASAMS) began in the 1980s as a replacement for the Cold-War HAWK missile. Norwegian company Kongsberg Defence and Aerospace worked in cooperation with US company Hughes, which was later acquired by Raytheon. The system entered full service in 1998 and is still in production.

The system uses a ground-launched variant of the US Advanced Medium Range Air to Air Missile (AMRAAM). The latest upgrade can also fire the AMRAAM-ER (Extended Range) and a ground-launched version of the AIM-9X Sidewinder, a US infrared seeking missile. Both missiles are widely used globally. The system also uses a Raytheon-produced radar system which can detect targets out to 80 miles, a German electro-optical sensor and a Norwegian fire control system called the Fire Distribution Centre (FDC). The launcher carries six missiles and can be mounted on a truck or a towed trailer.

BELOW: An AMRAAM missile flies from its launcher. A major advantage of the system is its use of proven missiles and components. (KONGSBERG AEROSPACE AND DEFENCE)

NASAM Missile System Characteristics	
Country of Origin	Norway/United States
Maximum Range	30km (18.64mi) AMRAAM 50km (31mi) AMRAAM-ER
Maximum Firing Altitude	21km (13.0mi) AMRAAM 35km (21.7mi) AMRAAM-ER
Missiles	6 per launcher

A key advantage for NASAMS is its interoperability with other air defence systems to act as part of an integrated air defence system. A full battery has 72 missiles in a dozen launchers and can track and engage multiple targets simultaneously. The FDC can integrate with the Patriot system, also in use by Ukraine. Patriot can handle long-range engagements while NASAMS can handle closer threats and whatever gets past the Patriots.

The United States has committed to providing eight NASAMS batteries to Ukraine, though six of those are to be new production, with two delivered from existing American stocks. Those batteries arrived in November 2022.

Though actual numbers are hard to confirm, the system has been successful against Russian UAS and missiles during the Russian aerial offensive against Ukrainian infrastructure. A US military report stated NASAMS had a 100% hit rate against Russian missiles during the 15th November, 2022, attacks on Ukraine's energy grid.

Ukraine appears to have moved a few NASAMS launcher closer to the front lines, enabling them to range against Russian close air support aircraft. It also makes them vulnerable to destruction, as the Russian were able to destroy one with a missile in late February 2024.

WEAPONS OF THE UKRAINE WAR

MANPADS

Man Portable Air Defence Systems

MANPADS Characteristics

Weapon	Igla	9K333 Verba	FIM92 Stinger	Starstreak	Mistral
Origin	Soviet Union	Russia	US	UK	France
Weight	17.9kg (39.5lb)	17.3kg (38.1lb)	15.7kg (34.6lb)	14kg (30.9lb)	19.7kg (43.4lb)
Target Ceiling	3.5km (2.17mi)	4.5km (2.8mi)	3.5km (2.17mi)	7km (4.3mi)	3km (1.86mi)
Range	4.1km (2.5mi)	6.5km (4mi)	4.5km (2.8mi)	7km (4.3mi)	6km (3.7mi)
Speed	Mach 1.9	Mach 1.5	Mach 2.2	Mach 4	Mach 2.71

BELOW: Many MANPADS can be mounted on a stand for easier use. This is a French Mistral in use by the Ukrainian 3rd Tank Brigade. (UKRAINIAN MOD)

Shoulder-fired anti-aircraft missiles are extensively used by both sides in the Ukraine War. Smaller than conventional surface to air missiles, MANPADS can still bring down aircraft and helicopters or damage them sufficiently to force the pilot to abort their mission. The presence of MANPADS also forces strike aircraft to fly higher, generally above 3,500 meters, which reduces the accuracy of their ordnance when not firing precision weapons. The major MANPADS used in Ukraine are:

Igla/Igla-S: This Soviet-designed weapon entered service in 1983 and is assigned the NATO reporting name SA-18 Grouse. It is used by both armies in Ukraine. The improved Igla-S entered service in 2002, incorporating a new seeker head, larger warhead and addition of a proximity/contact fuse. It also has a laser sensor which detonates the warhead when it is 1.5 m from the target, which makes it more effective against UAS.

9K333 Verba: This Russian weapon succeeded the Igla-S. It has a multispectral optical seeker which detects targets in ultraviolet, near and mid-infrared. The Verba can discriminate between targets and decoys and resist other countermeasures. It entered service in 2015 and is called the SA-29 Gizmo by NATO.

FIM92 Stinger: This US-designed missile entered service in 1981. Thousands have been supplied to Ukraine from several nations. Stingers have proven very effective in the Ukraine War. The missile is also mounted on the US built Avenger air defence vehicle, which Ukraine operates. There have been complaints from Ukrainian troops that some of their issued Stingers didn't work properly because they are past their shelf life.

Starstreak: The UK's Starstreak can achieve Mach 4, making it the fastest MANPADS in service. The warhead contains three tungsten darts with explosive charges which home in on the target after separating from the rocket motor. Starstreak can strike a target evading at nine Gs at seven kilometer altitude. It is immune to infrared and radar jamming.

Mistral: This French missile is operated by two soldiers as a normal MANPADS or as part of a Mistral Coordination Post (MCP) linking several missile units together to defend entire military units or important sites. The Ukrainians often position them around critical infrastructure to protect against UAS.

ABOVE: Multiple MANPADS can be mounted on a vehicle, increasing firepower. This British Stormer vehicle carries eight Starstreak missiles. (UKRAINIAN MOD)

UNMANNED SYSTEMS

Bayraktar

Unmanned Combat Aerial Vehicle

RIGHT: This TB2, named Vanagas 02, is a gift from Lithuania. Note the sensor dome just behind the front landing gear.
(LITHUANIAN MOD)

The Turkish-built Bayraktar TB2 unmanned aerial system (UAS) is another of the Ukraine War's well-known weapons, particularly in the conflict's early days. UAS have been in use since the 1960s, but in the 21st Century technological advances have allowed them to proliferate across battlefields worldwide.

Before the Russian invasion of Ukraine in 2022, the TB2 already built a reputation during the 2020 Nagorno-Karabakh War between Armenia and Azerbaijan. Ukraine contracted for 54 of them before the war and has received more since. A few have been purchased through crowdfunding efforts, including foreign contributions.

Bayraktar is capable of reconnaissance, target acquisition and artillery spotting. It can also carry out strikes using the MAM micro munition, a small precision missile effective against armoured vehicles and defensive positions. MAM is guided by a laser seeker and has a range of 15km. It can carry armour-piercing, high explosive fragmentation, and thermobaric warheads.

BELOW: A Ukrainian TB2 carrying a MAM missile on one of its external hardpoints. MAM is a Turkish acronym which translates to "smart micro munition."
(UKRAINIAN MOD)

The TB2 is also an economical option. An American MQ-1 Predator costs about $40 million not including any Hellfire missiles. A TB2 is $5 million, with 100 MAML munitions costing about $15 million more. The Turkish manufacturer, Baykar, is planning to build a factory in Ukraine.

Since neither side has been able to establish air superiority or dominance, TB2s remain effective on the battlefield. Ukraine has used them against Russian tanks and vehicles since the beginning of the war, often focusing against air defence systems and fuel transports. When Russian vehicles were stuck in long convoys outside Kyiv, they made particularly good targets for the Bayraktar. It is believed TB2s were used as decoys against the Russian cruiser *Moskva* when it was attacked by Ukrainian cruise missiles and later sunk after an ammunition explosion. They also attacked Russian patrol boats and weapons emplacements on and around the now-famous Snake Island.

However, as Russian air defences improved, TB2s became more vulnerable; advanced anti-aircraft weapons can easily engage the relatively slow-moving Bayraktar. The Russians proved able to down a considerable number of them. In response the Ukrainians have become more careful in the use of their TB2s, using them for strikes, surveillance and target acquisition only when conditions are favourable.

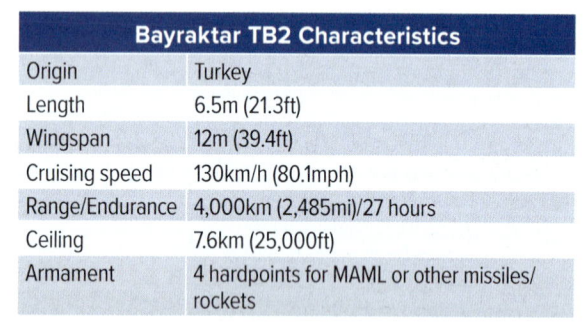

Bayraktar TB2 Characteristics	
Origin	Turkey
Length	6.5m (21.3ft)
Wingspan	12m (39.4ft)
Cruising speed	130km/h (80.1mph)
Range/Endurance	4,000km (2,485mi)/27 hours
Ceiling	7.6km (25,000ft)
Armament	4 hardpoints for MAML or other missiles/rockets

WEAPONS OF THE UKRAINE WAR

Shahed/Geran drones

Iranian kamikaze drone

The Shahed 131 and 136 drones are among the more well-known and reported UAS of the Ukraine War. They appeared unexpectedly in Russian service in late 2022, causing Western media and intelligence organisations to investigate the supply of Iranian weapons to Russia. Shaheds are also in use in several conflict areas in the Middle East. Remains of Shaheds from each area were compared, showing the drones in Ukraine were the same type. Russia has since built its own factory for producing the Geran 1 and 2, as it calls the Shahed. Iran states it supplied Shaheds to Russia before the current war began.

The Shahed 131 (Geran-1) is the smaller of the two types, shorter ranged and with a smaller warhead. The -131 is easily distinguishable from the -136 by the small vertical stabilisers at the end of the wings; in the -131 these stabilisers only project upward from the wings. Despite its shorter range and smaller warhead, the Shahed 131 is used in the Russian missile and drone offensive against Ukraine's infrastructure. A UK-based investigative group, Conflict Armament Research, discovered the -131's warhead was modified with 18 smaller charges around it and the addition of small metal particles to increase its damage potential.

The larger Shahed 136 (Geran-2) launches from a rack holding 5 drones. It uses a rocket assist for take-off; once airborne the rocket drops away and the drone proceeds using a rear-mounted propeller engine based on German technology acquired by Iran through espionage. Its long range allows it to be used on targets far behind the front lines and it is also frequently used in combination with missiles to strike Ukrainian infrastructure.

Ukrainian air defences are capable of downing Shahed drones and frequently do so, but mass attacks can overwhelm the defences, allowing some to reach their targets. With Russia able to produce them domestically and purchase them from Iran, the Shahed series will remain a common sight over Ukraine.

Shahed/Geran UAS		
	Shahed 131/Geran-1	Shahed 136/Geran-2
Origin	Iran/Russia	
Mass	135kg (297lb)	200kg (441lb)
Wingspan	2.2m (7.2ft)	2.5m (8.2ft)
Cruising speed	Unknown	185km/h (114mph)
Range	900km (559mi)/	2,500km (1553mi)
Ceiling	5,000m (16,404ft)	Unknown
Warhead	15kg (33lb) explosive	30-50kg (66-110lb)

ABOVE: When Shahed UAS first appeared in Ukraine, they were compared to known Shaheds recovered in the Middle East. These Shahed 131s formed part of the proof offered that Iran supplied Russia with these drones. (US DEFENSE INTELLIGENCE AGENCY)

LEFT: The Shahed 136 is launched from a rack system with rocket assist. This launch system provides the ability to get many Shaheds in the air quickly, providing mass numbers for an attack. (IRANIAN MOD)

www.keymilitary.com 95

UNMANNED SYSTEMS

Eleron-3

Russian reconnaissance UAS

ABOVE: Like the Orlan, the Eleron is recovered after a mission by deploying a small parachute. The small orange flag atop the parachute aids the operator in spotting the Eleron as it descends and lands. (RUSSIAN MOD)

Russia acquired several new UAS systems in the late 2000s and early 2010s. Among them is the Eleron 3, a reconnaissance drone originally marketed for civilian purposes. The Russian military saw the military potential in the design and adopted an upgraded version, the Eleron-3SW. Eleron is the Russian word for 'aileron,' a flight control surface used on fixed wing aircraft.

Eleron's payload is modular, allowing it to carry optical imaging, radio jamming or relay devices as needed. The imaging payload allows the user to pinpoint targets using either the Russian GLONASS or American GPS systems, enabling the Eleron to be used for targeting.

Like other UAS, the Eleron is susceptible to enemy fire, jamming and electronic warfare. Several have reportedly been downed using anti-drone rifles, such as the Lithuanian EDM4S, which is particularly effective against the Eleron. Despite this issue, the Eleron is one of the more common Russian UAS in the skies over Ukraine and continues in service.

RIGHT: Ukrainian special forces soldiers with an Eleron-3 they captured during a raid. The compact Eleron can be easily transported and used by frontline troops. (UKRAINIAN MOD)

BELOW: The Eleron's wings fold for storage and transport. This photograph was taken by Ukrainian special forces troops after capturing the unit intact. (UKRAINIAN MOD)

Eleron-3 UAS	
Origin	Russia
Mass	5.3kg (11.7lb) maximum takeoff weight
Wingspan	1.47m (4.82ft)
Maximum speed	130km/h (80.7mph)
Range/Endurance	60km (37.2mi)/ 100 minutes
Ceiling	4,000m (13,123ft)
Payloads	Optical and thermal imaging cameras, radio relay or jamming units available

WEAPONS OF THE UKRAINE WAR

Orlan

Versatile Russian UAS

The Orlan-10 is a Russian-made UAS developed in the late 2000s and entering full service in the mid-2010s. It is one of Russia's primary drone systems. Production has reportedly been dramatically increased to keep pace with battlefield demands.

A key advantage of the Orlan is its versatility. While relatively small, the Orlan's modular payload concept allows it to be equipped for different missions depending on need. There is an optical camera for observation and reconnaissance by the user, with modules available for electronic warfare, jamming and intelligence gathering. The Orlan also carries a laser rangefinder and other sensors to help direct artillery fire and precision weapons.

A radio transmitter allows the Orlan to differentiate between friendly and hostile transmissions. It can also jam cellular signals. The user can control the Orlan remotely or let it fly autonomously. It is launched via a small, portable catapult and is recovered using a parachute. Orlans can also be fitted with a kit to carry four small bombs, developed from 40mm grenades. The drone's flying altitude and inability to hover make it an inaccurate weapons delivery vehicle, however. It is much more effective in the reconnaissance and targeting roles.

Orlans are often used by Russian artillery units to deliver rapid strikes; Russian artillery often requires up to 20 minutes to deliver accurate fire on a target. A unit using the Orlan can reduce this to as little as three minutes. It is also a survivable system. A UK Royal United Services Institute assessment states the Orlan flies above the effective ceiling on MANPADS missiles but is small and inexpensive enough to be a difficult and not-cost effective target for larger air defence systems. This makes it more difficult to destroy, though Ukrainian troops have managed to down around 200 of them. It is believed the Russians operate over 1,000.

Downed Orlans have been found with Western components, leading to media investigations in 2023 as to how these electronics have been smuggled into Russia despite sanctions. It is an effective platform and Russia will make efforts to keep it in production.

Orlan-10 UAS	
Origin	Russia
Mass	15kg (33lb) maximum takeoff weight
Wingspan	3.1m (10.2ft)
Cruising speed	150km/h (93mph)
Range/Endurance	110km (68.3mi)/ 16 hours
Ceiling	5,000m (16,404ft)
Armament	Optional ability to carry four 40mm grenade-based bomblets

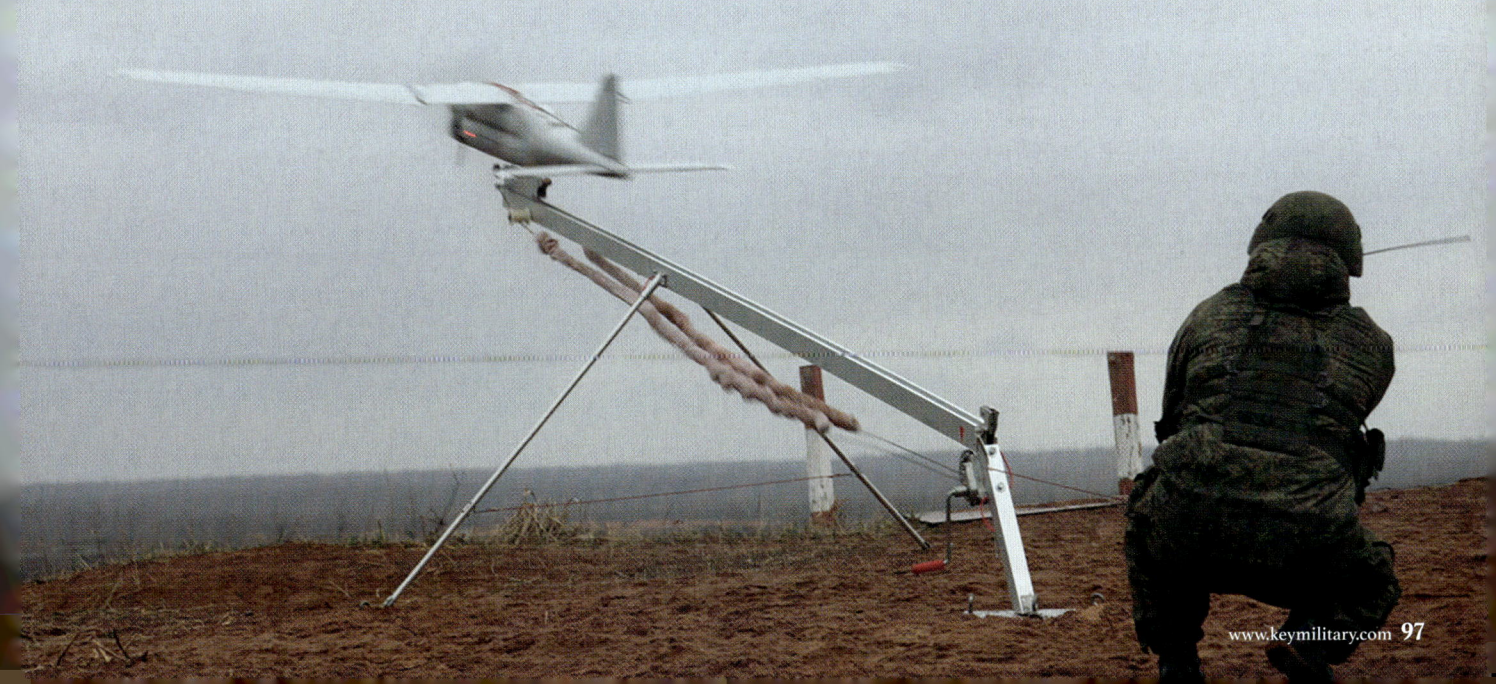

BELOW: The Orlan-10's control unit includes a simple laptop computer and what appears to be a device similar to a video game controller in the operator's hands. The use of such controllers simplifies training in the video game age. (RUSSIAN MOD)

BOTTOM: A soldier of the Russian 9th Guards Artillery Brigade launches an Orlan-10 UAS using its catapult. Upon returning from its mission the Orlan deploys a small parachute allowing it to be recovered for future use. (RUSSIAN MOD)

www.keymilitary.com 97

UNMANNED SYSTEMS

Small Drones

Inexpensive and versatile

RIGHT: This well-kitted Ukrainian soldier has a small quadcopter drone to provide overwatch. Such drones give troops on the front lines unprecedented situational awareness.
(UKRAINIAN GROUND FORCES)

Drone use in conflict has been steadily expanding since the 1960s, but the Ukraine War is the first where the world is seeing drone use by both combatants on a wide scale. This points to the future of warfare as soldiers are constantly innovating new uses for drones across the spectrum of military operations.

There are several reasons for the proliferation of drones in the Ukraine War:

Neither side has achieved air superiority. Large, manned aircraft are expensive, difficult and time consuming to replace as well as easy to defend against. Both sides suffered heavy aircraft losses in the beginning of the conflict. Russia has an air force far superior to Ukraine in numbers and quality, but it has failed to seize control of the skies and has been cautious in their risking of aircraft. Ukraine's smaller air force cannot afford to risk their aircraft except on the most important missions. Small, inexpensive drones allow both sides to carry out strikes, reconnaissance and target acquisition at lower cost and risk.

Drones are versatile. Small drones can be used down to the squad

BELOW: This publicity photo shows a shipment of drones in front of a display of captured Russian equipment. These drones will be used for artillery scouting and target acquisition.
(UKRAINIAN GROUND FORCES)

98 WEAPONS OF THE UKRAINE WAR

WEAPONS OF THE UKRAINE WAR

Russia has its own drone models and factories, but due to sanctions has some difficulty obtaining certain components. They have adapted by partnering with Iran, particularly on larger drone types such as the Shahed (see page 95) which have the range and carrying capacity for strike missions.

Small drones offer much, but there are numerous ways to defend against them. They are lightweight and relatively fragile, so a hit from a bullet or anti-aircraft cannon shell can easily bring them down. Some soldiers on the frontlines are using shotguns to down drones akin to skeet shooting. Anti-drone guns are rifle-sized electronic weapons which emit a jamming signal that can bring a small drone down. Various methods of electronic warfare, such as jamming and spoofing can cause a drone to crash, turn around, or fly off course. Small drones are more vulnerable since their size prevents them from carrying sophisticated anti-jamming devices. There is constant effort to develop new ways to stop drones and to defeat existing methods.

Despite these vulnerabilities small drones continue to proliferate on the battlefield. Ukraine is estimated to be losing 10,000 drones a month, but the benefits they provide far outweigh the losses and expense. New tactics are devised, and soon after counters to those tactics appear. The troops innovate and find a new way which is then eventually countered in an ongoing cycle with real-time feedback to users and manufacturers. Such cycles are not new in warfare, but they are happening much more quickly.

LEFT: Drones are a very modern technology, but old methods of shooting them down are among the most effective. These Ukrainian National Guard troops are using a 1960s-era ZU-23-2 antiaircraft gun against a drone strike in December 2023.
(UKRAINIAN NATIONAL GUARD)

LEFT: Russian troops are equally as innovative in drone use. These quadcopters carried explosive charges in attacks on Ukrainian positions. These drones did not complete their mission but many others do.
(UKRAINIAN NATIONAL POLICE)

BELOW: Anti-drone guns are also effective, particularly against small drones, such as this Russian Grifon reconnaissance drone brought down in October 2022.
(UKRAINIAN NATIONAL GUARD)

level, providing soldiers on the battlefield with their own scouting and observation abilities. Those same drones could be used to drop a grenade or explosive charge on an enemy position or carry a small amount of medical supplies to a wounded soldier. First person view drones, often used in filmmaking and drone racing, are fitted with explosives and sent on one-way missions against enemy forces. Small drones can be used to intercept larger drones by colliding with them.

Small drones are inexpensive.

Military hardware is costly, but many small drones are commercial models adapted to military purpose. Crowdfunding and donations are used in Ukraine to acquire drones, nicknamed 'dronations.' Civilian 'drone clubs' allows citizens to support the war effort by building drones. They are also relatively easy to manufacture quickly; Ukraine has over 80 drone manufacturers in early 2024, up from seven a year earlier.

www.keymilitary.com

UNMANNED SYSTEMS

Tupolev 141/143

Improvised ordnance

RIGHT: A Tu-143 roars from its launcher. The small jet under the fuselage is used to assist with take-off. They are recovered by parachute when used in the scouting role. (UKRAINIAN MOD)

Built as reconnaissance drones for the Soviet military, the Tupolev 141 and 143 entered service in the 1970s. Both are equipped with jet engines and are similar in design and appearance, though the Tu-141 is larger. When the Soviet Union dissolved, Russia and Ukraine inherited those remaining within their borders.

Obsolete in the 21st Century, Ukraine kept their Tupolev drones in storage until 2014. After the fighting began in the Donbass, Ukraine took some Tu-143s out of storage and used them in the reconnaissance role in Eastern Ukraine. At least two were shot down by Separatist forces.

Once the 2022 war began, Ukraine took more of the aging but still serviceable drones from storage and restored them. The Russians did the same, and both sides have apparently used them in the reconnaissance role, though it is unknown if either military updated or replaced the drone's Cold War-era camera systems.

BELOW: A Ukrainian Tu-141 is prepared for launch as a target drone in 2021. As a weapon it can do considerable damage but is vulnerable to a range of anti-aircraft systems. (UKRAINIAN MOD)

Before the war, both sides used them as target drones, the Ukrainians as recently as 2021. In the current conflict, both are also using them as decoys, sending them up against enemy air defence systems to distract them from other aircraft or UAS operating nearby. If the air defence system fires on the decoy drone it will possibly reveal its location for another asset, such as a loitering munition or a UAS directing artillery.

Ukraine, short on missiles and offensive ordnance, has also modified these drones into missiles, replacing the cameras with a warhead. The Ukrainian military has been discouraged from using Western-supplied ordnance against targets within Russian borders. Modifying leftover Soviet drones presents no such concern, however. The Tu-141 in particular possesses long-range, giving it the ability to strike targets deep with Russian territory. Proof of this appeared in March 2022, when a Tu-141 veered off course and crashed in Croatia with evidence explosives were on board.

In December 2022 these weapons were used in a strike on two Russian air bases, reportedly damaging three bombers and causing some other damage. Other attempts have been less successful as the drones were either shot down or jammed by Russian forces.

Tu-141/143 Characteristics		
Type	Tu-141	Tu-143
Weight	6,215kg (13,702lb)	1,230kg (2,712lb)
Length	14.33m (47ft)	8.06m (26.4ft)
Wingspan	3.08m (10.1ft)	2.24m (7.4ft)
Ceiling	6,000m (19,685ft)	5,000m (16,404ft)
Range	1,000km (621mi)	200km (124.2mi)
Speed	1,000km/h (621mph)	950km/h (590mph)

WEAPONS OF THE UKRAINE WAR

MAGURA Sea Drone

Maritime Autonomous Guard Unmanned Robotic Apparatus

Ukraine developed this innovative Unmanned Surface Vehicle (USV) during the present conflict as a low cost, effective and innovative solution to one of the nation's wartime challenges. The Russian Black Sea Fleet is far superior to the Ukrainian Navy. Ukraine lacks a navy able to fight the Russians. Instead, the nation must find alternate methods of neutralising Russia's maritime advantages.

This USV is a small, stealthy boat packed with sensors and explosives. It is often referred to as a 'Sea Drone' or 'Kamikaze Drone' though they have been seen with the name 'Sea Baby' on the hull. They are paid for through a crowdfunding initiative run by Ukraine's UNITED24 program. Each USV is said to cost $250,000. Some donors have even named the drone they paid for, such as 'Crime and Punishment' and 'Raccoon's Revenge.'

UNITED24 stated the USV has a range of 800km, giving a combat radius of 400km. Maximum speed is 80kph and it carries up to a 200kg (440lb) combat load. Other sources report the craft carries over 300kg (700lbs) of explosives. It has 60 hours of autonomous endurance and can be guided using GPS, inertial guidance or visual control. Its sensors enable the USV to carry out surveillance and reconnaissance missions or spot for other weapons such as artillery, missiles or UAS. A larger version able to carry a warhead five teams larger was unveiled in March 2024.

First use of these USVs occurred on 29th October 2022, when a combined force of aerial and sea drones attacked the Russian fleet anchorage at Sevastopol in Crimea, damaging three ships. The BBC estimated 13 separate attacks by Ukrainian USVs by September 2023. Other attacks have occurred at the Russian port of Novorossiysk and Chernomorske in Crimea. Ukrainian authorities say a July 2023 attack on the Kerch Bridge, which connects Russia to Crimea, involved two USVs. Another was used against the Russian intelligence ship *Ivan Khurs* in the Black Sea. Several struck and sank the amphibious ship *Caesar Kunikov* off the Crimean coast in February 2024. As of this writing, the Russian corvette *Sergei Kotov* was reportedly attacked and sunk on 4-5th March 2024.

ABOVE: This still image taken from video shows a USV closing in on the Russian ship *Ivan Khurs*. In the video it appears to reach the Russian ship. (UKRAINIAN MOD)

BELOW: This image shows the USV's antenna and optical systems, used to guide it to the target. The small circular shapes on the USV's bow are believed to be impact detonators. (UNITED24)

www.keymilitary.com

LOITERING MUNITIONS

Switchblade

Loitering munition

RIGHT: Switchblades launch from a tube similar to a mortar. Its name comes from the way its wing flips out from the main body as it launches. (US MARINE CORPS)

This loitering munition is a small, portable weapon system designed to be carried at the platoon level. It was intended to provide on demand fire support for small units which could not wait for artillery or air strikes. Originally developed for special operations forces, the Switchblade first saw combat in Afghanistan in 2012.

The Switchblade launches from a small tube using compressed air. It is equipped with a camera the user can monitor, providing reconnaissance capability. The user does not fly the Switchblade, but rather informs the munition what they want to observe or attack and the Switchblade directs itself as needed. They can cruise looking for targets and that target can be changed during flight. Switchblades are small and quiet; they can be hard to detect. They have a cruising speed while searching and a sprint speed when attacking.

The United States provided two versions of the Switchblade to Ukraine. The first is the Switchblade 300, an anti-personnel variant. It carries a small warhead equivalent to a 40mm grenade with pellets, akin to a large shotgun round. When it reaches the target this charge explodes, spraying the pellets forward rather than in a 360-degree pattern, reducing the danger of collateral damage. It is effective against personnel and unarmoured vehicles.

The Switchblade 600 is a larger, heavier system with an anti-armour warhead based on the Javelin missile. As it dives on the target it is capable of top attack against the thinner roof armour. After launch both munitions are controlled using a tablet and antenna. If no target is found, the Switchblade can be recovered for later use.

Ukraine received around 700 Switchblade 300s in Spring 2022 and began to receive the Switchblade 600 in late 2022. The 300 model has been used against fuel trucks, trenches and machine gun positions. Video exists showing Ukrainian Special Forces reportedly attacking Russian Tor air defence vehicles with Switchblade 600s.

	Switchblade Munition	
	Switchblade 300	**Switchblade 600**
Origin	United States	United States
Mass	2.5kg (5.5lb)	29.5kg (65lb)
Length	49.5cm (19.5in)	1.5m (60in)
Range	10km (6.2mi) or	40km (24.8mi)
Operating Altitude	150m (492ft)	198m (650ft)
Speed	101km/h (63mph) loitering 160km/h (100mph) sprint	113km/h (70mph) loitering 185km/h (115mph) sprint
Endurance	15 minutes	40 minutes
Warhead	Explosive fragmentation	15 kg (33 lb) anti-armour

BELOW: A Switchblade 300 in flight. This image shows the camera mounted at the front and the propeller at the rear of the munition's body. (US MARINE CORPS)

WEAPONS OF THE UKRAINE WAR

Lancet

Effective Russian loitering munition

Lancet Munition	
Origin	Russia
Mass	12kg (26.5lb)
Range	40km (24.8mi)
Speed	80-110km/h (49-68mph) loitering 300km/h (186mph) sprint
Endurance	40 minutes
Warhead	Explosive, Explosive fragmentation or Explosively Formed Penetrator (EFP)

The Lancet, produced by the ZALA Aero Group, is a loitering munition available in several versions. It entered service in the Russian Military in 2020 and production has since been increased due to the high demand for them in Ukraine. They first saw combat in Syria.

It is similar in many respects to the US Switchblade, as they perform the same function. It is propelled by a pusher engine at the rear and has eight wings in an X-shape. It has an optical guidance system the user can use to observe, scout, or assign targets. Lancets are also capable of autonomous attack.

The weapon has an endurance of 40 minutes and a range of 40km, although several targets have been struck farther from the front lines. This indicates either an extended range upgrade or that those attacks were launched by soldiers able to penetrate into Ukrainian rear areas. Spetsnaz troops could carry out such a strike as the Lancet is light enough to be carried by soldiers.

The Lancet is typically armed with a high explosive or fragmentation warhead, making it dangerous to exposed troops or lightly armoured vehicles. There is a heavier version able to attack tanks. Lancets are often used against artillery weapons, air defence systems, radars and other high-value targets. Ukrainian soldiers often rig chain link or wire netting around their vehicles to pre-detonate the Lancet's warhead.

In November 2023 reports appeared of Lancets armed with Explosively Formed Penetrators (EFPs). This type of warhead has an explosive charge behind a small metal plate. When the charge explodes, the plate is heated and curves into a slug which penetrates the target. To properly form the charge needs to detonate around 3-4 metres from the target. Lancet has a small laser rangefinder which would detect the optimum distance and trigger the explosion. EFPs can penetrate chain or wire netting and remain effective.

Lancet is a very effective weapon for the Russian military. However, an explosion at a manufacturing plant near Moscow the previous summer reportedly slowed or stopped Lancet production, though it is unknown for how long. Ironically, the highest praise for it comes from Ukraine, which announced on 7th February 2024 it was seeking its own version of the Lancet.

LEFT: This still captured from video shows a Russian Lancet loitering munitions attacking a Ukrainian MiG-29 fighter. Video from an observing UAS showed the Lancet strike the pavement just to the right of the cockpit area, likely damaging but not destroying it. (RUSSIAN MOD)

LEFT: This view of a captured Lancet drone shows the eight-wing configuration and the camera in the nose. (UKRAINIAN MOD)

MISSILES

Iskander

Precision-capable ballistic missile

ABOVE: An Iskander roars from its launch vehicle. A Russian rocket brigade can salvo 24 missiles at once. (RUSSIAN MOD)

The Iskander is a short-range ballistic missile system used by the Russian military for tactical and operational-level missions. It is more sophisticated than the Tochka, which is also used in the Ukraine War. It is more accurate and can be launched on short notice against targets of opportunity.

9K720 Iskander Missile Characteristics	
Origin	Russia
Mass:	3,800kg (8,400lb)
Length:	7.3m (24ft)
Warhead	480-700kg (1,060 – 1,540lb) HE-Fragmentation, submunition, earth penetrator, thermobaric or nuclear
Range*	500km (310mi)
Speed:	2000m/s (Mach 5.9)

*It is believed range is increased to as much as 1,000km with lighter payloads.

RIGHT: A loading truck reloads the Iskander TEL. They can be ready to fire again in as little as 21 minutes. (RUSSIAN MOD)

A basic Iskander launch unit contains a Transporter-Erector-Launcher (TEL) vehicle which carries two missiles. The TEL is supported by a command-and-control lorry and a data processing vehicle. A loading vehicle along with maintenance and crew support lorries complete the unit. Each battalion has four such launch systems, providing the ability to launch eight missiles in a single strike. Three battalions are further organized into a brigade. One or more brigades are assigned to each of Russia's military districts.

The brigade has further command vehicles able to receive and process targeting information. The TEL can be ready to fire in 16 minutes if it is moving, or five minutes if it is stationary. The missiles can be launched within one minute of each other and can be timed to arrive simultaneously. TEL's can be reloaded in 16 minutes. The system can launch several types of cruise missiles in addition to the Iskander.

The missile is intended for use against headquarters, ammunition depots, production facilities and other critical targets. It's reported accuracy is 5-10 meters, giving it precision capability. Iskander is designed to fly above the interception altitude of air defence systems like the Patriot but below that of ballistic missile interceptors.

The Ukraine War began with the Iskander. Within an hour of Russian President Putin's announcement that his forces were entering Ukraine, Iskander missiles fell on command posts, airports, ammunition depots and communications nodes. Later in the war the Iskander showed its ability to strike mobile targets when it was used to attack a Buk-M1 air defence vehicle.

WEAPONS OF THE UKRAINE WAR

Kinzhal Missile

Hypersonic or just ballistic?

The Kinzhal missile sees frequent use by Russia in the Ukraine War. There is controversy surrounding the weapon; Russia states it is a hypersonic weapon which can travel at Mach 10 and is virtually impossible to intercept. Some Western analysts claim the Kinzhal is just a modified Iskander which flies at Mach 5. Ukraine states it has shot down many Kinzhals using the US-supplied Patriot missile. In one interview, Ukrainian Patriot users claimed the Kinzhals they engaged were only moving at about Mach 3.6. Both sides dispute the other's statements, making it difficult to determine the facts. This is an excellent example of information operations in action!

Whatever the case, Kinzhal is a proven weapon frequently used in Russian missile attacks. It is a heavily modified Iskander with small manoeuvring fins. The MiG-31K supersonic interceptor is its launch vehicle. The MiG carries a single missile per sortie, flying at supersonic speed to an altitude of 18 km. The pilot releases the Kinzhal, which separates about 30 meters from the aircraft before its solid fuel rocket motor activates.

Once in flight the Kinzhal quickly accelerates to Mach 4 on the way to its maximum speed. The missile's range of 2,000km includes the 1,000km combat radius of the MiG-31.

The Kinzhal can be equipped with a concrete piercing warhead for use against underground bunkers. Like the Iskander, the Kinzhal's warhead is believed capable of manoeuvring in the terminal phase of flight. This may explain the lower speeds observed by the Ukrainians, as a manoeuvring missile will tend to shed velocity.

There are claims the Russian Tu-22M bomber can carry four Kinzhals, but this is disputed since it is slower than the MiG-31K and its service ceiling is below the Kinzhal's 18km launch altitude.

The Kinzhal is frequently used in attacks against infrastructure such as command centres, production facilities, and infrastructure. Missile strikes on Kyiv and Kharkiv often include the Kinzhal. The first announced combat use of the missile came on March 18-19, 2022, against a munitions depot near Deliatyn in southwestern Ukraine.

Kinzhal Missile Characteristics	
Origin	Russia
Mass	4,800kg (9,500lb)
Length	8m (26.2ft)
Warhead	480kg High Explosive
Range*	2,000km (1,243mi)
Speed	Up to Mach 10 per Russian Government
* Range includes MiG-31K range of 1,000km	

ABOVE: This image taken from a Russian Ministry of Defence video shows a Kinzhal just after launch. The missile's solid fuel rocket motor is about to activate, sending the weapon on a ballistic trajectory. (RUSSIAN MOD)

LEFT: A MiG-31K interceptor carrying a Kinzhal missile. The similarity to the Iskander missile is apparent in this view. (RUSSIAN MOD)

MISSILES

KH-101

Stealthy Russian cruise missile

RIGHT: A KH-101 missile shot down in Vinnytsia in January of 2023. The pointed nose is designed to lower the radar signature of the weapon. (UKRAINIAN AIR FORCE)

BELOW: A Tu-160 launching a Kh-101 missile at a target in Syria, 2015. The bomber can carry up to 12 Kh-101s in its internal weapons bays. Note the bomber is escorted by an Su-30 fighter. (RUSSIAN MOD)

The Kh-101 is derived from the Kh-55 series of cruise missiles developed by the Soviet Union in the 1970s. Design work began in the Soviet Union in the late 1980s and was continued by Russia in the 1990s. Typical of weapons development in the cash-starved Russia of that period, the design process was extended, with the Kh-101 entering full service in 2012. It is armed with a conventional warhead; the Kh-102 is a nuclear-armed variant with a 250 kt warhead.

The air-launched Kh-101 is a stealthy missile with a low radar cross signature. Composite materials are used in its construction which absorb radar waves, making the Kh-101 difficult to detect. While it cruises at 6,000 metres it can drop to low altitude to avoid enemy radar, as low as 30-60 metres. The missile has terrain following guidance and also uses GLONASS, the Russian version of GPS. During its final approach to the target, it uses a television imaging infrared seeker.

It is typically carried by bombers such as the Tu-95, Tu-22 and Tu-160, but can also be fitted to large strike aircraft such as the Su-27 and Su-34. Warheads include high explosive, cluster/submunition and earth penetrating. The missile is reportedly capable of updating its course mid-flight and operators can even change its target in flight if needed. The Kh-101 is an accurate weapon, able to typically strike within 10-20 metres of its target.

The Kh-101 saw extensive use in Syria, beginning soon after an attack by the so-called Islamic State upon a Russian airliner, killing 249 people. The missiles targeted headquarters, ammunition depots and other high-value targets. The missile also sees frequent use against Ukraine, also targeting important sites including airports, air bases and infrastructure. The weapon's long range allows it to be fired from the Russian side of the border, keeping the launching aircraft away from Ukrainian air defence systems.

Some Western analysts have stated Kh-101 missiles suffer large amounts of malfunctions, causing them to miss their target or fail to detonate. The Russian are also using their older Kh-55 missiles and other older models as decoys fitted with inert warheads to overwhelm and distract the Ukrainian air defences.

KH-101 Missile Characteristics	
Origin	Soviet Union/Russia
Mass:	2,400kg (5,291lb)
Length:	7.45m (24.4ft)
Warhead	450kg (992lb) - conventional warhead
Range	2,800km (1,739mi)
Speed:	0.78 Mach (598mph)

WEAPONS OF THE UKRAINE WAR

WEAPONS OF THE UKRAINE WAR

Kalibr Cruise Missile

Russia's versatile precision weapon

The Kalibr is another missile system frequently mentioned in the media. It is used often in Russian missile attacks on Ukrainian infrastructure and high value targets, such as around Kyiv and Kharkiv. It is comparable in most respects to the Tomahawk missile in service with the UK and US Navies. It is not a new weapon, having entered service in 1994.

Kalibr is designed to function day or night, in any weather. Targets are typically static installations such as airfields, port facilities, logistics depots, command posts and bridges. There is also a version which can engage submarines. The Kalibr can be launched by ground vehicles, aircraft, surface ships and submarines.

The Russians frequently use ships of the Black Sea Fleet to fire the Kalibr. Surface ships generally use vertical launch tubes while submarines fire from the torpedo tubes. The Kalibr's range, estimated at 1,500km, allows Russian vessels to launch attacks from outside the range of Ukrainian shore-based defences. It can also be launched by the SU-35 fighter and Russian bombers.

Once launched, the Kalibr flies low, about 20 metres over water and 30-150 metres over land, dropping to 20 metres when nearing the target. Speed is high subsonic, though a booster can be fitted to some versions to achieve supersonic flight. The onboard guidance system uses inertial navigation, a radio altimeter and satellite navigation. The missile's flight path is predetermined using target location and intelligence on air defences.

The initial Russian missile strikes in the first hours of the war included Kalibr cruise missiles. Ukrainian statements point to their frequent use against their power grid. In July 2022 Russian naval forces fired four Kalibrs at the port of Odessa. Russia claimed to hit a Ukrainian naval vessel while the Ukrainians stated two missiles were shot down while the other two hit a fuel pumping station.

It appears to be an effective weapon, though each side makes differing claims as to its accuracy. There is also dispute over how many Kalibrs Ukrainian air defences have been able to shoot down. This is normal during a conflict; accurate statistics are generally not available until the war is over, if ever.

Kalibr Missile Characteristics	
Origin	Russia
Mass:	1,770kg (3.902lbs)
Length:	6.2 - 8.9m (20.3 – 29.1 feet)
Warhead	Estimated 450kg (992lb)
Range	Estimated 1,500km (932mi)
Speed:	0.8 Mach standard, supersonic boosters exist

ABOVE: A Kalibr missile made this crater outside a Ukrainian naval facility in Mykolaiv on 27th April, 2023. (UKRAINIAN NATIONAL POLICE)

LEFT: A Kalibr missile is launched from the Russian Buyan-class corvette *Vyshniy Volochyok*. This ship is reportedly in the Black Sea Fleet and has eight vertical launch tubes for Kalibr missiles. (RUSSIAN MOD)

MISSILES

R-360 Neptune

Ukraine's homemade anti-ship missile

RIGHT: A Neptune missile launcher with its command vehicle, trucks carrying reload missiles and other support vehicles.
(PRESIDENT OF UKRAINE)

Ukraine has limited naval power and its navy is dwarfed by the Russian Black Sea Fleet. This presents a difficult situation for Ukraine, as it must defend an extensive coastline from naval attacks and amphibious assaults where their opponent can concentrate power at a given point.

One of Ukraine's answers to this dilemma is the R-360 Neptune missile. This domestically produced weapon is based on the Soviet designed, Russian built Kh-35, but the Ukrainian version has a larger booster and longer body for more fuel.

Before the break with Russia, Ukraine built engines and other parts for the Kh-35 and possessed the technical information for it. Initial testing of the Neptune occurred in 2016 with further development and trials through 2020. It was funded for production in 2021 with plans to field 18-19 launchers in 2022.

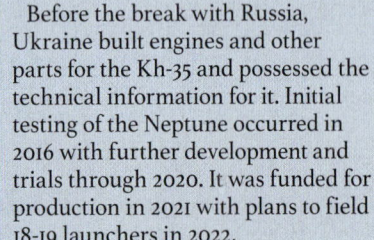

BELOW: A Neptune missile flies from its launch tube. A launcher must be within 25 miles of the coast for a sea attack. The threat of weapons like the Neptune keep Russian naval vessels at a greater distance from shore.
(UKRAINIAN MOD)

R-360 Neptune Missile Characteristics	
Origin	Ukraine
Mass:	870kg (1,918lb)
Length:	5.05m (16.6ft) when deployed for firing
Warhead	150kg (331lb) HE-Fragmentation
Range	300km (186mi)
Speed:	900km/hr (559mph)

After launch the Neptune cruises 10-15 metres above the surface until it nears the target, when it descends to 3-10 metres to avoid air defence weapons. A Neptune battery typically has six launchers with 24 missiles and takes 15 minutes to be ready to fire.

Ukraine states it first used the Neptune in early April 2022 against the Russian frigate Admiral Essen when it was cruising near the Ukrainian port city of Pivdennyi with several Russian landing craft. The Neptune is most famous for the sinking of the Russian cruiser Moskva in April 2022. Two missiles struck the ship, which subsequently suffered an apparent ammunition explosion and sank. Moskva is one of the largest naval vessels sunk since World War II. It has also been used in several other attacks, often in concert with other weapons such as UAS.

The Ukrainians announced they were perfecting a land attack version and in August 2023 stated Neptunes were used in attacks on the Crimean Peninsula against Russian defences. This includes a Russian S-400 surface to air missile unit. During the war the Russians have purposefully targeted Neptune production facilities. It is uncertain how this has affected Ukraine's ability to manufacture the Neptune.

WEAPONS OF THE UKRAINE WAR

Storm Shadow

Advanced cruise missile

Storm Shadow is another Western weapon which has received extensive media attention on its provision to Ukraine. It is also the topic of extensive information operations as each side makes claims about its effectiveness. Like the HIMARs and Kinzhal, for example, whatever is said on social media and news reports, Storm Shadow has proven itself effective.

This cruise missile is a joint Anglo-French product equipping British and French forces since 2003. It is a long-range precision weapon able to strike stationary targets such as command posts, runways, bridges, bunkers and ships in port. It uses a combination of inertial guidance, GPS and terrain matching to accurately reach its target. An imaging infrared seeker activates during final approach. It also compares its programmed impact point to the actual site using target recognition algorithms.

Storm Shadow employs a tandem warhead, using two detonation stages to help in penetrating underground or hardened structures such as reinforced aircraft hangars. Prior to the Ukraine War, Storm Shadows saw use in Iraq, Libya and Syria. This weapon gives Ukraine a counterpart to various cruise and ballistic missiles in Russian use. It gives Ukraine a long-range capability it previously lacked.

The missile is air launched, but Ukraine does not operate any of the Western aircraft which carry it. Instead, Storm Shadow has been retrofitted onto the Su-24M tactical strike plane flown by the 7th Tactical Aviation Brigade. Each Su-24M can carry two missiles. The Russians naturally target this unit, which habitually disperses to avoid incoming strikes.

Several notable strikes have involved Storm Shadow missiles. A strike in June 2023 damaged the road bridge between Crimea and Kherson. A month later another Storm Shadow damaged a railroad bridge in the same area.

In September 2023, multiple strikes hit the Russian Black Sea Fleet in Sevastopol, damaging two naval vessels and striking the fleet headquarters; the Ukrainians stated this attack targeted the fleet's leadership. In December another strike hit the Russian landing ship *Novocherkassk*, effectively destroying it.

LEFT: Ukrainian President Volodymyr Zelenskyy inscribes a Storm Shadow missile during an Air Force Day ceremony in August 2023. Successful missile strikes provide boosts to Ukrainian morale. (OFFICE OF THE PRESIDENT OF UKRAINE)

Storm Shadow Missile Characteristics	
Origin	UK/France
Mass:	1300kg (2,900lb)
Length:	5.1m (16.7ft)
Warhead	450kg (990lb)
Range	550km (340mi)
Speed:	Mach 0.95

BELOW: The Russian landing ship Novocherkassk burns in Feodosia port in Crimea after a strike using Storm Shadow missiles. (UKRAINIAN MOD)

ELECTRONIC WARFARE

Electronic warfare

A constant unseen struggle

RIGHT: Russian soldiers set up a MKTK-1A EW vehicle, which specialises in radio frequency detection, direction finding and analysis. One downside to such systems is need for easily observable antennae, allowing them to be targeted. (RUSSIAN MOD)

It would be difficult to overstate the importance of Electronic Warfare (EW) on the battlefields of Ukraine. It performs many roles, including jamming or spoofing of GPS signals, radio communications, drone guidance and satellite connection. Spoofing is an EW technique which tricks a weapon such as a drone or missile into thinking it is somewhere else, causing it to miss its intended target.

EW systems come in many varieties and sizes. They are fitted on aircraft including helicopters, vehicles, ships and even small handheld devices soldiers can carry with them. New devices, often improvised in the field, are tested constantly and both sides are in a constant cycle of design, use and adaptation.

Russia has a clear superiority in EW. The military reforms began in 2008 focused on EW as a way to level the playing field with the West, which enjoyed a clear advantage in precision guided weapons, UAS and advanced electronics. This effort paid dividends as the Russians have used this capability since the seizure of the Crimea and the 2014-15 Donbass War.

Jack Watling of the UK's Royal United Services Institute has spoken to the widespread Russian use of EW systems, stating "...the Russians are able to field electronic warfare systems across most of the front, down to platoon level in some cases." The Russians are having success in jamming the signals of Western ordnance, such as HIMARS rockets, the Switchblade loitering munition and the Excalibur 155mm guided artillery round.

While Ukraine struggles to compete in the EW realm, it has achieved some successes. Some of their domestically developed systems are able to block the guidance of Russian missiles and drones. If a Russian EW system is spotted setting up, efforts are made to destroy it before it becomes active. Just before a 2023 missile attack on the Black Sea Fleet at the Russian-held port of Sevastopol, Ukrainian special forces disabled Russian EW systems mounted on an offshore oil platform, enabling the strike.

RIGHT: Ukraine's Nota EW System disrupts radio networks, jams signals and locates radio transmitters. Matching Russian EW capabilities is a constant challenge and Ukraine has greatly increased its ability to produce such systems. (UKRAINIAN GENERAL STAFF)

WEAPONS OF THE UKRAINE WAR

Mines

A deadly and enduring threat

Landmines are in widespread use across the battlefield. Both anti-personnel and anti-vehicle mines are common. Mines are generally laid in front of defensive positions to make it more difficult for an attacker. They are also laid to protect flanks, slow an enemy force or direct them in a direction you want them to go, allowing you to place fire on them. Troops caught in a minefield must move slowly and cautiously, making them more vulnerable to incoming artillery and small arms fire. Vehicles immobilised by mines can be attacked by helicopters or anti-tank teams. The Russians notably used these techniques to slow the Ukrainian counter-offensive in the second half of 2023.

Anti-personnel mines use a combination of blast effects and fragmentation to inflict casualties. Anti-vehicle mines (often called anti-tank mines) use blast effects. Anti-vehicle mines often immobilise vehicles rather than destroy them. Mines can be activated by pressure (stepping or driving on it) or a tripwire. A few mines have sensors which detects approaching footsteps.

Landmines are one of the great tragedies of the Ukraine War. They are indiscriminate, affecting civilians and soldiers alike. When the frontlines move, the minefields are usually left behind, posing a hazard to anyone in the area. Large amounts of mine clearing equipment have been sent to Ukraine. It will take years, if not decades, to clean up all the minefields once the war is over.

ABOVE: The PTM1-G is a scatterable mine dropped by helicopter or using rocket artillery such as the BM-21. It is plastic bodied and can be set to self-destruct up to 24 hours after being deployed. (UKRAINIAN STATE EMERGENCY SERVICES)

LEFT: Mines can be laid underwater, usually at shallow fords and crossing points. These are Soviet-era TM-62M anti-tank mines. (UKRAINIAN STATE EMERGENCY SERVICES)

BELOW: These PNM-4 mines were discovered under a farm road near Sumy. The PNM-4 is one of the most common landmines in the world and has been widely copied. (UKRAINIAN NATIONAL POLICE)

www.keymilitary.com

MINES

Mine Clearing
Dangerous and stressful work

ABOVE LEFT: These anti-mine overboots are used by demining personnel in Ukraine. They limit contact with the ground and provide a short stand-off distance to allow a mine explosion to dissipate. (UKRAINIAN NATIONAL POLICE)

ABOVE RIGHT: Dogs are also used to locate mines. Patron is a mine location dog who has won awards from Ukrainian President Zelenskyy and the Irish Kennel Club for his work locating mines and unexploded ordnance. (UKRAINIAN STATE EMERGENCY SERVICES)

RIGHT: Metal detectors are commonly used to clear mines in Ukraine. Models such as this CEIA can also detect wires, mercury switches and some non-metallic devices. (UKRAINIAN MOD)

RIGHT: The Russians are fielding a series of unmanned, robotic military vehicles. These Russian engineers are following an Uran-6 sapper robot, which can survive blast of up to 60kg of explosives. (RUSSIAN MOD)

112 WEAPONS OF THE UKRAINE WAR

WEAPONS OF THE UKRAINE WAR

Black Sea Fleet

Russian naval power

One of Russia's greatest advantages over Ukraine is the size and strength of its Black Sea Fleet. This force far outnumbers and outguns the much smaller Ukrainian Navy. While the world's focus has concentrated mainly on the fighting on land, the Black Sea Fleet plays an important part in Russia's war effort.

There are two main ways in which the Black Sea Fleet influences the war. First, its missile-equipped ships and submarines take part in the frequent attacks on Ukrainian military, industrial and infrastructure facilities. Weapons such as the Kalibr cruise missile (see page 107) can be launched from naval vessels. There are reports that anti-aircraft and anti-ship missiles have been modified for attacking land targets.

Second, the fleet's large number of amphibious warfare vessels present a threat to the entire Ukrainian coastline, enabling a landing of troops behind Ukrainian front lines or an attack on a port city like Odessa. This threat forces Ukraine to assign resources to coastal defence which it needs elsewhere. Even if no landing is planned, the possibility forces preparation against it. Amphibious ships are also used to move supplies to Russian troops ashore.

Ukraine has no realistic chance to engage and defeat the Black Sea Fleet but can force it to stay away from the coast. To do so it has created a strong coastal defence force equipped with US Harpoon and Ukrainian Neptune missiles, backed by UAS and air support. Several Russian ships, including the fleet flagship, the cruiser *Moskva* have been lost to missile attacks and several others to unmanned suicide boats (see page 101). This has so far compelled the Russian fleet to stay farther out to sea. Each missile ship sunk or damaged is one less to launch attacks and each amphibious ship lost reduces Russia's ability to carry out a landing or carry supplies.

Despite some Ukrainian successes, the Black Sea Fleet remains a major threat, even when acting as a fleet in being. Its firepower and ability to move troops cannot be ignored.

Ship Strength of the Black Sea Fleet

Type	Number	Notes
Frigates	5	1 reported damaged in October 2022
Corvettes	17	2 reported sunk or damaged, 1 damaged
Attack Submarines	7	1 damaged while in dock
Missile Boats	5	1 sunk, these are like a missile corvette in capability
Patrol Boats	4	2 reported damaged, 1 possibly sunk
Minesweepers	13	1 reported damaged
Anti-Saboteur Boats	15	1 reported destroyed, up to 7 damaged or destroyed
Amphibious Ships	16*	At least 2 sunk, several damaged, reports conflict
Intelligence Ships	4	1 sunk or damaged
Auxiliaries	8	5 Oilers, 1 Logistics Vessel, 2 Repair vessels,
Survey Ships	3	

* Five amphibious ships were moved to the Black Sea Fleet in early February 2022

The Black Sea fleet also controls coastal defence, missile, air defence, aviation, naval infantry and special forces units.

ABOVE: *Burya*, a Project 1241 *Molniya*-class missile boat, is assigned to the Black Sea Fleet. It alone would be a challenge for any of the Ukrainian Navy's ships. (RUSSIAN MOD)

LEFT: MT-LB personnel carriers move down the ramp of a Russian landing ship. The amphibious warfare ships of the Black Sea Fleet could in theory land a brigade-sized force. (RUSSIAN MOD)

Glossary
Acronyms and terms

AFV: Armoured Fighting Vehicle
AK: Avtomat Kalashnikov, Soviet/Russian rifle series
AMRAAM: Advanced Medium Range Air to Air Missile
APC: Armoured Personnel Carrier
APFSDS: Armour-Piercing Fin-Stabilised Discarding Sabot, an anti-armour round used in tank guns
ATACMS: Army Tactical Missile System
ATGM: Anti-Tank Guided Missile
BTG: Battalion Tactical Group, the basic Russian combat unit
CAA: Combined Arms Army (Russian)
CLU: Command Launch Unit, aiming device for the Javelin missile
DPICM: Dual Purpose Improved Conventional Munition
EFP: Explosively Formed Penetrators
ERA: Explosive Reactive Armour, a type of add-on armour
EW: Electronic Warfare
FDC: Fire Distribution Centre (air defence) or Fire Direction Centre (artillery)
GLONASS: Russian satellite navigation system
GLSDB: Ground-Launched Small Diameter Bomb
GPMG: General Purpose Machine Gun
GPS: Global Positioning System
GTD: Guards Tank Division
HEAT: High Explosive Anti-Tank
HIMARS: High Mobility Artillery Rocket System
HMG: Heavy Machine Gun
HQ: Headquarters
IADS: Integrated Air Defence System

IFV: Infantry Fighting Vehicle
LAW: Light Anti-tank Weapon
LMG: Light Machine Gun
MANPADS: Man Portable Air Defence System
MBT: Main Battle Tank
MLRS: Multiple Launch Rocket System
MoD: Ministry of Defence
NASAMS: Norwegian (sometimes National) Advanced Surface to Air Missile System
NATO: North Atlantic Treaty Organisation
NBC: Nuclear-Biological-Chemical
NLAW: Next-Generation Light Anti-Tank Weapon
NCO: Non-Commissioned Officer
OK: Operational Command, Ukrainian regional headquarters
OMON: Mobile Special Purpose Detachment, Russian paramilitary force
OSK: Operational Strategic Command, Russian regional military headquarters
RAP: Rocket Assisted Projectile
Rosgvardia: Russian National Guard
RPG: Rocket Propelled Grenade
RWS: Remote Weapon Station
SAM: Surface to Air Missile
SPG: Self-Propelled Gun
TEL: Transporter-Erector-Launcher
UAS: Unmanned Aerial Systems
USAF: United States Air Force
USV: Unmanned Surface Vehicle
VDV: 'Vozdushno Desantnye Voyska,' Russian Airborne Forces

PHOTO CREDITS:
Bulgarian MoD, Iranian MoD, Kongsberg Aerospace and Defence, Lithuanian MoD, Netherlands MoD, Office of the President of the Russian Federation, Office of the President of Ukraine, Poland MoD, Russian Air Force, Russian MoD, UK MoD, Ukrainian Air Force, Ukrainian Air Assault Forces, Ukrainian General Staff, Ukrainian Ground Forces, Ukrainian Joint Forces Command, Ukrainian Ministry of Internal Affairs, Ukrainian MoD, Ukrainian Navy, Ukrainian National Police, Ukrainian State Emergency Services, UNITED24, US Defense Intelligence Agency, US DoD, US Air Force, US Air National Guard, US Army, US Marine Corps, US Navy.

BELOW: MANPADS are widely used by both sides against aircraft, helicopters, UAS and missiles. Many nations are trying to increase their stocks of these weapons after seeing the numbers of them used in Ukraine. (UKRAINIAN MOD)